THE JESUS I KNOW

Edited by Adam Harbinson

The Jesus I Know

the columba press

First published in 2009 by
the columba press
55A Spruce Avenue, Stillorgan Industrial Park,
Blackrock, Co Dublin

Cover by Bill Bolger
Origination by The Columba Press
Printed in Ireland by ColourBooks Ltd, Dublin

ISBN 978-1-85607-654-8

Table of Contents

Introduction

My friend, the author and evangelist J John, tells the story of an occasion when he was in conversation with a neighbour who claimed to know nothing of Jesus. No surprise perhaps, for we do live in what some see as a post-Christian era. But the astonishing thing is that having said he would give his neighbour a book about Jesus, J John couldn't find one. None in his extensive library and none in the numerous bookshops he scoured in an attempt to keep his word. So he went home and wrote one – as you do! And so was born his book, *The Life* published by Authentic – so now there's at least one good book about Jesus.

It could perhaps be said that Philip Yancey's excellent book, *The Jesus I Never Knew* is a book about Jesus, but it's more about who Jesus is not, for Yancey, telling of his own appalling experience of the fundamentalist church of his childhood says, 'I was an angry, wounded person emerging from a toxic church, and I've been in recovery ever since.'

Many Christians, myself included, can easily relate to Yancey's experience. Some, like him, went through a period of complete rejection of all things religious, only to meet the real Jesus in later life. I have met many such people who long to tell of the Jesus they have come to know. One is my friend Alan Abernethy, Bishop of Connor. The idea of this book was partly his, and you will find his moving story in these pages. But then he went on to write a further two chapters that allow Lord Eames (retired Archbishop of Armagh and Primate of Ireland) and Mark Simpson (BBC Ireland Correspondent) to tell theirs too.

I have been warmed and inspired as I've worked on the book; almost forty people, some high profile personalities, others who will never have their fifteen minutes of fame. Some will make you laugh, and some will make you cry, but each contributes their own unique portrait of Jesus. Each individual image is a jigsaw piece in a much bigger picture, but put them all together and there emerges a wonderful kaleidoscope of the characteristics of Jesus the Servant King, the Good Shepherd, the faithful friend who sticks closer than a brother, the one who says, 'I will never leave you.'

But in his time, this Jesus was regarded as an itinerant preacher from a backwater village. He never went to university, never owned a home, never wrote a book, did not have a place to lay his head, was vilified, and died an ignominious death on a Roman cross. Surely it's absurd to suggest that the teachings and example of such a man could have any relevance for people who live in a foreign land with an alien culture and a different language two thousand years after his death? Did he really rise from the dead and with his band of unlikely followers change the world for ever?

My hope and prayer is that as you read these stories from a handful of his twenty-first century followers, the living Jesus will leap off the pages and become real to you. He can bring you comfort and peace in a world of turmoil and fear. He can bring you courage and strength to face your demons however frightening they may be. And he can shower you with the full measure of his reckless, unconditional love.

The real Jesus changed the world forever; he can change your world forever too.

My thanks to each of the contributors. Without their willing co-operation this book would not have been possible.

Adam Harbinson 2009

Foreword

By Charles Badenoch
CEO World Vision UK

It's Saturday morning, the end of a busy week and I am sitting at Glasgow airport waiting to fly home to my family. I groan inwardly as I remember that I must write the foreword for the book *The Jesus I Know*. I start to read the manuscripts and my groans turn to joy as I am once again reminded about the Jesus that I, and millions of others throughout the ages and around the world, are so blessed to know. So I strongly recommend that you read and re-read the chapters of this book whenever the day to day grind of life wears you down and leads you to forget about the Jesus you and I know. For those of you who do not yet know Jesus, I strongly urge you to read this book and discover what you are missing.

The Jesus I know is always with me even though many times I ignore him or turn my back on him and go my own way. I am a stubborn person and for many years I did not listen to Jesus when he was trying to guide me in a certain direction. Fortunately, some three years ago I did listen to Jesus when he called me out of my life in the commercial sector to join the Christian international relief and development agency World Vision UK as Chief Executive. Through this new job I have been privileged and humbled to meet so many incredible people all over the world who are following Jesus' command to love their neighbour by walking alongside and loving the poor, the marginalised and the socially excluded, just as Jesus did 2000 years ago.

In this book you will read many moving personal accounts about the Jesus that they know. Nigel Bovey writes about 'the Jesus I know is a down to earth Jesus' who 'is not concerned about what people think of him. He wants to make those who think they are nobody realise that in his eyes – and in the opinion of his Father – they are somebody.' Jesus hangs out with the most stigmatised members of society – the Jesus I know embraces and loves all those with HIV and AIDS, the mentally and physically disabled, the criminals, the terrorists, the Dalits.

Conrad Gempf talks about 'that voice and the way that when he calls my name it puts a lump in my throat – all that love and warning and disappointment and encouragement all at once. And I fumble for the iPod, not sure whether to turn it off or up.' Are we prepared to create the space in our busy life to intentionally listen to Jesus in the many ways he talks to us? And when we listen, are we prepared to hear and act? Listening to, acting and following Jesus is not comfortable. In fact, it is risky. Gordon McDade gives ten reasons why knowing Jesus involves risky living. And he concludes his thoughts on *The Jesus I Know* with a quote from an anonymous poem which sums up for me a difficult truth: 'Only a person who risks all he cannot keep, to gain that which he can never lose, is truly free.'

Many readers will be able to relate to Adam Harbinson's reflections on *The Jesus I Know*. Adam vividly contrasts the man-made image of Jesus that he suffered through childhood, with the real Jesus that he 'bumped into in later life and fell in love with'. In childhood Adam was introduced to a man-made 'all seeing, all knowing, capricious killjoy'. The Jesus that Adam has come to know and love is inclusive, not exclusive. The Jesus Adam knows 'loves the military man or woman who releases the bomb from the F16, but you will find him on the ground too, cradling in his arms the dying child and the bleeding Muslim. He is not willing that any should perish, he wants all to know him and to share his love.'

Bishop Ken Clarke reminded me that we often overcomplicate Jesus. He recalls an early childhood experience where he learnt that Jesus 'helps us and that he is with us wherever we are'. Yes, Jesus loves me. A child's mind can understand this and the greatest minds in the world are humbled by this same simple truth. He loves us and he helps us because he loves us.

However, Ken goes on to remind us that Jesus' love is 'not a wishy-washy kind of love'. Jesus' love is 'a selfless muscular love'.

So, wherever you are in your journey of life, create the space and time to read and reflect on this book of treasures. I hope and pray that, by the time you come to the end, you will truly feel and believe that nothing can compare with *The Jesus I Know*.

Bishop Ken Clarke
Bishop of Kilmore, Elphin and Ardagh

When the Ghost Train broke down, Jesus could help me.
I was sure of that.

I will never forget my childhood experience of the Ghost Train breaking down in the darkness in Barry's Amusement Park in Portrush on the north Antrim coast. From waves of fear and from the very depth of my heart I cried out for divine help with utter sincerity and compelling urgency. One of the first lessons I had learned about Jesus was that he helps us and that he is with us wherever we are. Such convictions did not flow from extensive reading of the Bible, because I was too young to read. They flowed from the teaching of my parents. The first song I ever remember singing was one they had taught me. Unknown to me I had been learning theology from hymns and in this situation of stress and distress it rapidly became applied theology!

Jesus loves me this I know. For the Bible tells me so.
Little ones to him belong. They are weak but he is strong.
Yes Jesus loves me …

A child's mind can understand this and some of the greatest minds in the world are humbled by this same simple truth. He loves us, and he helps us because he loves us.

The Jesus I still know 50 years later is the same Jesus I knew then. Of course I no longer visualise him in long pristine white robes, immaculate flowing hair and surrounded by perfectly behaved children as he was in my first *Children's Book of Bible Stories*. But I now have a lifelong experience of his unique kind of love. The Jesus who walked on earth and the Jesus I know, is a Jesus whose love is a selfless muscular love. His love is not a wishy-washy, wimpish kind of love. His love is surprising in its expression, disturbing in its extent and profoundly overwhelming in my personal experience and the experience of millions of others across the nations and generations.

The Jesus I know is a trailblazer, courageous in his actions, astonishing in his attitudes, a breaker of moulds but always in line with his Father's will. He profoundly disturbs religious people. He constantly engages with needy people. He, a Jew, spoke with a Samaritan woman. When I was younger I had no idea of the revolutionary nature of this unusual encounter. In this meeting with the Samaritan woman he was crossing national, cultural, social and religious boundaries. He was walking where the strict religious Jews would not walk. He was building friendship where others would not. St John wrote that Jesus was, '... full of grace and truth'. Amazing, overflowing and never ending grace, which is loving and showing favour to those who do not deserve to be loved, marked his whole life. If we need anything at the beginning of the twenty-first century, we need to discover the Jesus of the gospels who reached out to all in his society and who forgave even his enemies. From the cross he prayed, 'Father forgive them for they know not what they do.' This is the Jesus who loved 'the other side,' the despised, the outcast, the misunderstood, the last, the least and the lost. This is the Jesus I am getting to know – and he disturbs me.

He challenges my prejudices. He calls me to be radical. He confronts my hypocrisy. He sees my secret struggles. He is hurt by my sin. Yet I still see the moisture of grace in his eyes and I still know the depth of his mercy in my heart. I have said sorry many times for my rebellion and folly. I recognise the reality of his forgiveness in my life. I hear him whisper in my ear, 'Your sins are forgiven. Go and sin no more.' They are, but I don't. The Jesus I have come to know forgives and forgives and forgives again. Like the apostle Paul I cannot get over the fact that he loves me and gave himself for me. It is an incredible thought but such a releasing truth. I know that the truth, his truth, sets people free.

To some this may seem strange, but the Jesus I know has enabled me to know a sense of rest and an ongoing restlessness. I have known peace but I can never settle. He constantly calls me to new adventures in my mind and life. He stretches me, and repeatedly in my inner being I hear his words, 'Follow me.' Following means change. Obedience is sometimes painful. He takes me where I am not sure I want to go. He leads me in the known and in the unknown. Yet the alternative is to miss out on what it means to be a disciple. In bereavement, disappointment and in those personal and family pains, which you are not sure you want anyone else to know about, I have known Jesus Christ. He is the Jesus of the cross and of suffering. He is the Jesus of resurrection and hope. The two are inseparable. The longer I know him the more convinced I am that his call to follow him is a call to suffering and glory. Heaven will be all glory. But that is yet to be.

The Jesus I know is the Jesus who knows me. I'm back where I started. I am still overwhelmed by his love as I travel on a different train, the train of mid-life. For this I have Jesus! The words of the following hymn have meant much to me in recent years:

For the joys and for the sorrows, the best and worst of times
For this moment for tomorrow, for what lies behind.
Fears that crowd around me, for the failure of my plans
For the dreams of all I hope to be, the truth of what I am.
For this I have Jesus.

For the tears that flow in secret, in the broken times
For the moments of elation or the troubled mind.
For all the disappointments, the sting of old regrets
All my prayers and longings that seem unanswered yet.
For this I have Jesus.[1]

1. Graham Kendrick © 1994 Make Way Music.
www.grahamkendrick.co.uk

BISHOP KEN CLARKE grew up in Holywood, Co Down, Northern Ireland where the formative influences on his life were his local parish church, Scripture Union and Crusaders. He is married to Helen and they have four daughters, four sons-in-law and four adorable grandchildren.

Ken has served in parishes in Northern Ireland, Chile with the South American Missionary Society, and in Crinken, Dublin. Before moving to his present diocese in January 2001 he was Rector of Coleraine parish for 15 years. He has led missions and preached at conferences and conventions in different parts of the world. He enjoys reading, supporting Manchester United, walking, golf, and has a particular interest in church growth and leadership issues.

Andy Chamberlain
Author and Pastor

*

I am writing this at a time of significant uncertainty in my spiritual life. I am dealing with an issue that took me out of pastoral ministry, and at the moment I am not really sure how things will work out.

It's not sex or money that's caused this; no one asked me quietly to step down. It's more about expectation: what I expect from God and what I think he expects from me. My contract with God is in tatters. It's a time of uncertainty, a time when I desperately need Jesus to strip away my defences and pretences, and deal with me: I expect it to be a rough ride.

And yet this is a very good place for me to be. It means that I am provoked into thinking about Jesus as I really know him; not as the God I am trying to impress, but as the Saviour of my soul.

If you are still wondering what my issue is, let me encourage you to take a deep breath and leave the question to one side; think rather of your own engagement with him. What is important is that Jesus is able to meet us at these times, and be real to us, whatever is happening in our lives. I know that as I take up my cross and walk, Jesus has already shouldered the burden. He has already carried it; he knows its weight, and the harsh rub of wood on skin; the Jesus I know has suffered everything that I will ever suffer, and much more.

The Bible frequently uses the metaphor of the refiner's fire to describe how God uses difficult times to purify us. The fire burns away the rubbish, leaving only those things that are real and true. We all know this, but the knowledge can sometimes be of small comfort when we are going through it. The Christian life necessarily involves a number of occasions when this process happens; and although I do not enjoy such times, I do welcome them as a check on my motivations and my work for God.

In his first letter to the Corinthians, Paul talks about our work being 'revealed with fire' as God tests the quality of what we do.

What will be left once God's fire has passed over my efforts for him? Will I scramble into heaven as a man runs out of a burning house? What about you, how will you fare when that moment comes?

These challenges reveal the truth about our motivations and the depth of our relationship with Jesus; and experience has taught me to identify three sources of truth about our Saviour, three ways to discover who he really is. These sources are: the scriptures, true worship, and what might be termed contending with Jesus.

Jesus in the scriptures

I got to know Jesus better through a simple reading of the gospel accounts. Most of us are familiar with reading portions of scripture for Bible study and sermons, but sometimes we need to simply read the narrative. In doing so we discover the 'story' of Jesus rather than have him presented to us in a considered way, as is the case with a sermon. Let me say straight away that there's nothing wrong with the concept of the sermon – I've preached a few myself – they are a wonderful way to engage with our scriptures. But the story of Jesus contains something that discrete chunks can't give us.

I found that our Messiah is a most dangerous person. The style of the gospels is spare and uncompromising, and the more I read, the faster the story moved; the narrator took me from one episode to the next to the next in a breathless series of engagements and confrontations. When you read about Jesus you find that at every point the motivations and vulnerabilities of the people around him are stripped bare. His analysis is uncompromising, his compassion is absolute, and his tolerance of pride is zero.

The Jesus I know treats me in the same way. If I approach him with any seriousness he begins to unnerve me. The Jesus of the scriptures is full of compassion, but for our own sakes he will not let us hide anything. He will not let us behave like an eloquent barrister playing to the jury, he won't let us put our stuff into context, present it as material suitable for viewing. There's none of that; rather he will find us out and lead us on as real people, not the pretenders we can so easily become.

Jesus in true worship

Just as Jesus had no time for pretence during his earthly ministry, so any serious attempt to worship him will also drive us to a painful reality. In a moment of candour, the Messiah told those who would listen that the greatest commandment is to love the Lord your God with everything you have – everything. We shall never really be satisfied with our own attempts to marginalise Jesus, to put him in a box, to say nice things about him and to him. Our worship, like our reading of the gospels, will be ruthless in finding us out, requiring our all, and forcing us to confront the real Jesus.

Contending with Jesus

In our struggles, we must either reject this real Jesus or discover him in a new and more profound way. This is especially true when we are confronted by pain and loss. We wrestle with the seemingly pointless tragedies of life; the wreckage of the way life treats people is all around us. Part of the brilliance of our faith is that he is also in the wreckage; and not as a visiting dignitary but as a victim, as one who has been there. Plenty of religions in the world either promise perfection or punish for the absence of it; these 'push-pull' belief systems wave the carrot or the stick, success or failure, in front of us. But the real Jesus isn't kicking us from behind or shouting at us from the front; he is there beside us, with us.

Pain makes us companionable with Jesus. When we contend we don't have the energy for pretence, he can do some serious business with us. It is in the pain that we can find Jesus. He is not the remote and indifferent God of other faiths; he has more than earned the right to receive our worship, even as we suffer. This is an important truth for all Christians to learn: we should not deny the anguish we feel – God does not ask us to be dishonest;

but in the midst of it we must still worship him, and indeed will feel authentic comfort in that.

When life is going well we can easily accommodate him; Jesus becomes another topic for conversation at the dinner table, another source of entertainment. But when we contend with Jesus we have to take him seriously. At such a time there is more at stake; there are our relationships, our precious resources: time, money, life. This is the level at which I find Jesus. He can not be boxed and packaged as a product. He smiles at the many good works we might use to authenticate ourselves. He is intimate with us in our struggle because this is the only way he chooses to engage with anyone. As I am real with him in my poverty and pain, so he will be real with me in his compassion and love. So as I think through my expectations of God, as I deal with my stuff, I am profoundly reassured: the Saviour I know will spare me nothing. I will have nowhere to hide, and so one day I will find myself in his fearful and wonderful love; this is the Jesus I know.

ANDREW CHAMBERLAIN has contributed to a number of Christian magazines and his novel *Urban Angel* is published by Authentic Media. From 2000 to 2007 he was Senior Pastor at the Cambridge Vineyard Church in England. He now worships in a local church in Cambridge with his family.

Gary Clayton
Managing Editor OMF International

*

> *The Jesus I know is one who redeems, restores and renews.*
> *The Jesus I knew – or thought I knew – was a troublesome Jewish guy*
> *who founded a new religion.*

As a Jew, albeit a fairly non-practising one, I sang the old play-ground chant, 'Roses are reddish, violets are bluish, if it wasn't for Jesus we'd all be Jewish' with the best of them.

In my mind, if Jesus – or *Yeshua*, as his contemporaries knew him – hadn't built a large following around his claim to heal and to forgive sins, Christianity would never have come into being. There wouldn't have been any Christians – only Jews. (At least at the North London school I attended.)

But although Christianity appeared to be an anomaly and an irrelevance, I wasn't that keen on Judaism either. Bar Mitzvah – the coming of age ceremony that occurs when a Jewish boy reaches 13 – seemed to have nothing to do with faith, but was all about going through the motions.

It didn't matter what any of us believed (Father Christmas, extraterrestrials, astral projection, yogic flying, whatever), as long as we attended synagogue the requisite number of times, learnt to read Hebrew and went to all the classes, we graduated.

The rabbi didn't help. Every Shabbat (Saturday) he smiled at his congregation whilst checking to see we were all present and correct, and talked of God's love. But during Hebrew class, he muttered something about breaking our necks whenever we were noisy – which didn't exactly inspire me! Something, I thought, doesn't add up here.

Then there was the car thing. On Saturday nearly everyone we knew drove to synagogue, even though it was the Sabbath and was against the rules. So, whether they came from near or far, most of the congregation parked their cars round the corner and walked the last half mile.

'And you walked all the way from the other side of town to be here,' said one of the few congregants who lived only a few streets away, and didn't have a car, 'You must be exhausted!'

I knew from scripture about the patriarchs, prophets, priests and kings, and that many of them had a close relationship with God. But that wasn't my experience. It was all about parking cars and not being caught. So if that was the reality, then what the Bible said must be sham.

'What,' I thought, 'if God doesn't exist? – I can do anything. I can even take an oath in his name, lie through my teeth and never get struck by lightning!'

But through a Christian friend who was actually Jewish, I was taken to an old synagogue where young Christians met, and soon realised I was wrong. Jesus existed. It didn't matter whether I was Jewish, atheist, Buddhist or Hindu – the only way to experience God and find salvation was through him.

But that was over 20 years ago. Since then I've discovered more about the Jewish roots of my faith, been published in various Christian newspapers and magazines, been on TV (don't ask!), travelled from Odessa to Israel helping Jewish people emigrate to the land of their forefathers, worked for three different Christian organisations, (films, then magazines and now OMF International), witnessed numerous church splits, and ministered with a man who later went off the rails.

Not content with declaring himself a prophet and king, this former Messianic Christian leader took up with seven women – 'wives' he called them – whilst still legally married to his original, much put upon, and later separated partner. Years earlier I had taken part in a conference he'd organised (I'd also helped him plan and promote it), and had spoken on the subject of 'False prophets'. With hindsight, I realise I shouldn't have addressed the audience – I should have made my remarks to him. (Of course I should also have recognised the signs I was so authoritatively speaking about ...)

But what about the Jesus who redeems, restores and renews? Well, as I said earlier, he redeemed me. He took me from being a cynical student who played 'Spot the Christian' at Manchester University (I laid bets that every gawky, freaky, geeky-looking individual we saw anywhere near the Christian Union was a Bible-bashing believer with a personality defect the size of the Grand Canyon) to being the Managing Editor of *East Asia's Billions*, the magazine originally edited by Hudson Taylor, founder of the China Inland Mission (now OMF), in the 1800s.

But Jesus also restored me. My bad experience with the guy who had fallen from grace took its spiritual toll, so work seemed a good way to channel my energies. Unfortunately Christian bosses can be as bad as secular ones (sometimes worse!), and can be so driven by ambition (presumably for the kingdom) that they'll drive their employees into the ground or up the wall.

I was in the right place but it all felt wrong. All I could do was grit my teeth, stick to my guns and not get fired.

So I turned my frustration and hurt over to Jesus, knowing that nothing I'd experienced compared with his sufferings – and prayed for strength. Eventually my hyper-perfectionist overcritical boss moved on and I was eventually promoted. Having redeemed me, Jesus restored me. But he also renewed me.

Although I had outlasted my old boss and had escaped from the ministry of a man who later spent time in jail, my confidence had taken a battering. The past hadn't exactly been a blaze of glory and the future, as my 30s began to trickle away, didn't seem to hold out much promise.

I kept on keeping on, but I was heading towards 40 and, having spent most of my time doing Christian things at the expense of building relationships, thought marriage had passed me by. (Some people can have seven 'wives', I thought. I can't even find one!) And then, amazingly, before I had time for a mid-life crisis (just!), I met Julie.

It was the last thing I was expecting, but thanks to God everything changed. Years later, I thank God for my loving wife, wonderful son and beautiful daughter. Being in my 40s isn't so bad. Hopefully the rest of my Christian walk will be free from the perils and pitfalls of the past.

The Jesus who redeemed me, restored me. The Jesus who restored me, has renewed me.

GARY CLAYTON comes from a nominal Jewish background and became a believer at 21. He studied English Literature at Manchester University, and spent a year looking for gainful employment before working for International Christian Films. After four years, Gary moved on to PWM as Managing Editor of Rev Dr Clifford Hill's *Prophecy Today* magazine (now *Sword*), running one of the UK's largest mainstream non-denominational magazines. In 1995, wanting further challenges, Gary joined OMF International (originally Hudson Taylor's China Inland Mission), producing the mission's magazine, prayer and promotional materials. He is married to Julie and has two children, Christopher and Emma.

The Jesus I grew up with was a tough, demanding Jesus. He insisted on me wearing my best clothes when visiting his house, the place where he lived. He didn't allow me to buy sweets on a Sunday. I could go for a walk with my grandparents but I couldn't ride my bike, nor could I kick a football. My hair had to be short and my sisters' hair had to be long, and when they went to visit him, they had to wear a hat, otherwise they would be unwelcome.

Life with this Jesus was a long series of rules: no cinema, only Christian music to be listened to, no modern clothes, girls must not wear make-up nor have long nails. There was a constant fear that I might upset the Jesus I thought I knew. I well remember stories of fathers forcibly snipping daughters' fingernails deemed to be Jezebel-like. Is it any wonder that I, with many of my peers, dumped him as soon as we had the freedom to do so? After all, who would want to spend a lifetime, not to mention eternity, with such an all-seeing, all-knowing, capricious killjoy?

But in later life I bumped into the real Jesus, and I fell in love with him. The big thinker! He was happy to spend time with me because he loved me ... that was my first surprise. He didn't judge me or punish me for my wrongdoings, not because he compromised or watered down his impossibly high standards, but because he had given me the gift of his righteousness.

I love the story of the two Chinese brothers. One was a degenerate, the other a quiet, studious Christian lad. The wild boy got into a fight and murdered his opponent. He rushed home, discarded his bloodied clothes and made his escape. His brother arrived home from a prayer meeting and discovered the clothes. When a loud knocking at the door signalled the arrival of the police, he added two and two. He donned his brother's clothes knowing they would incriminate him, and was led peacefully to the police station. In due course he was executed and when the murderer found out about his brother's fate he returned, tearfully, to the magistrate, demanding to be put out of his agony by being allowed to follow his loving brother. But the debt had been paid. That's what the Jesus I now know did for me.

The hymn writer, Toplady, knew the Jesus I know too. He wrote,

> Payment he will not twice demand,
> First at my bleeding surety's hand,
> And then again at mine.

The Jesus I know is in the business of redemption; he paid my debts and thus allows his Father to welcome me into the family. The Jesus I know does not point the finger and accuse, that's Satan's job. The Jesus I know weeps with me, laughs with me, enjoys my company, revels in fellowship with me. The Jesus I know goes before me, levelling my path and turns to me saying, 'This is the way,' but he will not force me to walk in it. The Jesus I know does not control me; he leads, guides, protects and feeds me, but he will always acknowledge my freedom to choose. And when I get it wrong, the Jesus I know will never say, 'I told you so'; rather, he stoops to wipe away my tears and bathe my self-inflicted wounds with oil and wine, and sets me on my way again. The Jesus I know loves the military man or woman who releases the bomb from the F 16, but you'll find him on the ground too, cradling in his arms the dying child and the bleeding Muslim. He is not willing that any should perish, he wants all to know him and to share in his love.

The Jesus I know has no favourites. He said, 'As the Father loves me, so I love you.' The Jesus I know is sometimes disappointed with his church, hurt when they drive people away, but yet he loves the church, his bride, dressed in spotless white. John the apostle demonstrated this when he penned the letter to the church in Laodicea. They had locked his Jesus out, but patiently he stood there, knocking at the door, offering friendship and pleading fellowship. The Jesus I know had equal status with God and yet for you and for me, he lived a selfless, obedient life and died a selfless, obedient death. The Jesus I know does not love cautiously, he loves extravagantly, and he wants us to do the same.

This is the Jesus I know.

ADAM HARBINSON is an author, speaker, lecturer, broadcaster and a newspaper columnist. He was born in Portadown, Co Armagh and now lives in Bangor in the beautiful Co Down in the north of Ireland. He is married to Pauline and between them they have seven children and four grandsons.

Adam's primary concern, expressed in all he seeks to do, is to help his readers and listeners to know that there's a difference between religion – defined as what people do *for* God – and the life of faith, which is based on a relationship *with* God. He believes that it is this relationship that informs and shapes how we see ourselves and how we interact with the world around us.

For more information visit: www.adamharbinson.com

Canon J. John
Evangelist and Author

●

When thirteen-year-old David was asked what he knew about Jesus, he replied, 'Why was he named after a swear word?'

Jesus. A name that stirs up such controversy, yet the reputation of this man has withstood scrutiny for 2000 years. Today, passing a high-street surfing shop, his name is branded across merchandise: *Jesus surfs without a board* and *Jesus is my homeboy*. A mark of our times, perhaps, that this name of such power and significance can be so casually thrown around. One step even further away from the assumption that this name will evoke extreme reactions: either a trust and acceptance of the biblical view of Jesus as God's Son or a sceptical view, belittling him to the category of a 'good man'. Now, it seems our culture has broken beyond that, allowing room for its use as a faint, lethargic gag and nothing stronger.

Knowledge of Jesus is commonplace, but can we say that we know Jesus? Certainly, few would deny his existence. Today, a growing body of fifteen hundred million people trace their faith back to this historical figure; historians can verify his existence against Roman records while theologians prove the validity of the gospels as an authoritative written account of Jesus' words and actions. We have evidence and confirmation that he lived in Palestine, that he was considered to be the Messiah and that he was executed under Pontius Pilate, who governed Palestine from AD 26 to 36. This was the man, a peasant teacher living on the edge of the map in Judea, who made an impression so big that the normal categories of history and biography did not seem enough and a new literary genre developed to do him justice. Still, can our knowledge of this man rest and lie dormant in historical accounts?

Reading the gospels, we can know of his life, his teachings and his miracles. This was no ordinary man. He was a man of such power, of peace and of love. This was the man who turned water into wine, drove out demons, fed the five thousand and walked on water. He gave his love and attention to an adulterous woman; he opened the eyes of a man born blind; he taught of his Father in heaven and he called us his friends. Crowds flocked to hear him. A sick woman strained for just a touch of his cloak. A leprous man knelt before him. Wind and waves obeyed his commands. He offered rest for the weary. At the cross, against every human instinct, he offered himself to God as a price for our sin.

This Jesus is a rather unsettling figure, who both comforts those who are troubled and troubles those who are comfortable. A man of love, but also radical, commanding and challenging. He tells the rich man that it is harder for him to enter the kingdom of God than it is for a camel to pass through the eye of a needle. He assures us that from those to whom much has been given, much will be demanded. The first will be last and the last will be first, and he professed that anyone who does not give up everything they have to follow him cannot be his disciple. And this is the man who asks us, one by one, 'Who do you say that I am?'

In 1998, my friend Lee Strobel, a journalist, wrote a book recording his investigation into the evidence of Jesus. He interviewed a scholar, analysed data, and studied the historical evidence, and the influence and effect that Jesus can have on one person's life

Having assessed all of the evidence, Lee, once a confirmed atheist, came to faith and trusted the evidence. Yet what is worth recording is not that he could muster sufficient evidence and facts to believe, but that when he did, his life changed. So much so that a few months after he became a follower of Jesus, his five-year-old daughter told his wife, 'Mummy, I want God to do for me what he's done for Daddy.'[1]

The knowledge and facts of the person of Jesus remain on paper, and yet it is this man's life-transforming impact on those who believe today that marks the Jesus I know. Unless Jesus'

1. Lee Strobel, *The Case for Christ*, Zondervan, 1998, p 269

transforming power is real today, he can be no more or less interesting than any other historical figure, than a Henry VIII or a Churchill. The difference lies in the fact that this Jesus is as real today as he is in the historical evidence and, moreover, he connects us to God. This Jesus shows us our God and has made it possible for us to have a relationship with him. 'If you really knew me, you would know my Father as well.'

The Jesus I know turns lives around and turns our world upside down. Faith in this Jesus gives us a depth and dimension that we cannot experience in any other way. This Jesus takes us, as we are, making us anew as we become children of God; 'The old has gone, the new has come'.[2] He heals bruised, broken and wounded lives, offering us forgiveness, blessing and guidance. He is the 'Bread of Life' who gives us food that sustains, and drink that quenches thirst, and he questions each one of us, as he did Simon Peter, asking, 'Have I not chosen you?'

Like pieces of a puzzle, we fit together a portrait of this man. The man, without 'beauty or majesty to attract us to him'. The 'man of sorrows', who was 'familiar with suffering',[3] and was despised and mocked by his people. A perfect, pure and holy man, a man of such care and compassion, who promises peace and commands us to 'take heart' for he has overcome the world.[4] He reveals to us the perfect nature of our God, the God who prepared, planned and pursues us, offering us life, his way, in all its fullness.

We are not called to always understand God's way, to fathom the mysteries that sometimes seem to shroud our universe, to master contemporary theological debate or even to experience a smooth and unchallenged road of faith. But we can look to this man, our beacon and guide, and recognise the simplicity of God in Jesus. Jesus is not complex or difficult to decipher – his message is simple and clear.

There is simplicity and peace in the Jesus I know. A man,

---

2. 2 Corinthians 5:17
3. Isaiah 53:3
4. John 16:33

demonstrating a life of love, who demands that we turn from lives that are wrong and follow his lead. A shepherd searching for his lost sheep – and for the thirteen-year-old David who only knows of him as a swear word – and he calls us to go in his name and to do the same.

J. JOHN is regarded as one of the most creative Christian speakers with an appeal that transcends gender, age, race, culture and oc-cupation. He communicates the timeless principles and values of the Bible and shows their relevance to our lives today.

J. John lives in Chorleywood, Hertfordshire in England. He is married to Killy and they have three sons, Michael, Simeon and Benjamin.

For more information visit: www.philotrust.com

Aidan Troy
Catholic Priest

It was St Valentine's Day 2004. Roses were in the shops and chocolates everywhere for those who wanted to say something of their love. That morning I stood at the graveside of a young man of 17 who had hung himself at home a few days earlier. It was awful. There were not any words to fill the gap of understanding or ointment to soothe the pain. It was as dark as Calvary. Worse was to follow on this Valentine's Day.

That afternoon the best friend of the young man we had buried that morning climbed the scaffolding of the Holy Cross Monastery Church and hung himself from the pinnacle of this imposing building in the heart of North Belfast. The church was celebrating 100 years and was undergoing extensive restoration work. I climbed the scaffolding – ladder after ladder and not daring to look down – until finally I saw the slight body of a young man hanging by the collar of his jacket. I shouted out a word. Silence came back to me. I prayed and kept talking to him in the hope that he was still alive. The boards began to creak as the emergency services arrived. One police officer took a real risk as he inched his way out to bring in the young man. All efforts to resuscitate him came to nothing.

I made my way down the ladders to be met by a huge crowd that had gathered. A man asked me what colour shirt the boy was wearing. I told him cream and blue. He said simply, 'That's my son.' It was an hour before the body could be brought down. I went into the back of the ambulance with the father and at once he cradled the body of his son. It was a most moving moment to see a tough and strong man weep salt tears as he cradled the broken body of his son.

In that moment I saw the face of God as Father looking on the face of his Son. That is how God loves us. This picture of Jesus as Son beloved by the Father will never leave me. The God of love revealed in Jesus cradles us, his children, in his arms.

* * *

William had a colourful career and had travelled all over the world. But eventually alcohol got the better of him. Each day I would see him at the corner of the street with a bottle beside him. I got to know him and he never let me pass without a word of greeting. I always felt guilty when I saw William lying in his own dirt but lacked the courage to do anything. Then one day a few local people asked if they could bring William to Holy Cross Monastery once a week for a bath. They bought clothes and on a Saturday night would bring him for his bath and dress him in his new clothes. William looked a million dollars after his bath and change of clothes.

As I watched these people bring William into our Monastery I couldn't but think of the words: 'Truly, I say to you, as you did it to one of the least of these my brethren, you did it to me' (Mt 25:40). The next day in the Eucharist I would utter with reverence, 'This is my body.' The vulnerability of Jesus was with me in the vulnerability of William. When William died recently he looked so young and at peace in his coffin. By that time I believe he was already with Jesus. William without knowing made Jesus powerfully real to me.

***

The twins were born prematurely. The parents soon realised that all was not well. Both were weak and the outlook was not great. But the parents have great faith. God would see them through. The day I baptised the twins in an incubator in a Belfast Maternity Hospital was a moving moment for the little group of believers as we received these little ones into our lives and our belief. The days ahead were tough, with hopes raised and then dashed. Then one of these little ones died. The other survived and is now a healthy one-year-old taking in all that is happening in his world. The burial of the little one was heart-rending. But the parents never flinched or blamed God. They told the other children about their new family member and still speak his name as easily as if were in the home with them.

When the disciples tried to keep the children away from

Jesus the rebuke was clear. 'Let the children come to me, do not hinder them; for to such belongs the kingdom of God' (Mk 10:14). In the vulnerability of the child, a wonder of God's creation, I caught a glimpse of the innocence and beauty of Jesus.

In 2001 a protest at a parish school in Holy Cross parish gave me a privilege to see the forgiveness and lack of bitterness that children are capable of showing. For months on end 225 small girls were caught up in events that no child should ever witness. At the end of months of the most awful events not one of those children showed any hatred or resentment. Some of us adults had to battle against a desire to retaliate and seek revenge. Not so the children, as they just asked why this was happening. They showed me a tolerance and a beauty that is of the kingdom. Jesus shone through them in their acceptance and lack of hitting back. I can now understand a little better why Jesus put a child in the midst of his followers who wanted to know about greatness in the kingdom. A child is the model and I am grateful to those little children for leading me to see this.

In his poem 'After Forty Years of Age'[1] Patrick Kavanagh reflects that: 'The job is to answer questions/Experience, [to] tell us what life has taught you.' In truth, the face of Jesus and the traces of his kingdom I have found all around me and often in the most unlikely and unpromising places. Without these my faith in Jesus would be difficult to sustain.

AIDAN TROY: Born in Bray, Co Wicklow and a priest since 1970 Aidan Troy's life was shaped by the faith of his parents and by the people he met along the way. Academic studies were important to him, but his radical formation came from young and old who taught him to believe, to hope and to love. He says that amazing blessings came upon him during his seven years at Holy Cross, Belfast: 'Children showed me the way of love; wounded people from all sides of a divided and hurt community taught me about forgiveness, and all have left me filled with trust in Jesus as Way, Truth and Life.'

1. Patrick Kavanagh, *Selected Poems*, Penguin Books, 1996, p 108

You can read Fr Aidan Troy's insider account of the horrors of the Holy Cross protest in his book: *Holy Cross – A Personal Experience*, available from www.currach.ie

Adrian Plass
Author and Speaker

·

One day a man called Denis Shepherd, from one of the London churches, came to speak to the evening congregation. He was a tall, broad man, with a quiet manner and an air of inner strength. As far as I can recall he had been in the Merchant Navy for some years before being ordained into the Anglican Church. I was still very much a spectator, and I would have rejected with scorn the suggestion that what this man said was going to bring real tears to my eyes and, for better or worse, change the whole course of my life.

The talk he gave was about the brief conversation between Jesus, as he hung dying on the cross, and the two lawbreakers who were crucified on either side of him, an event which is recorded only in the gospel of Luke. The preacher read the relevant passage before beginning his talk.

One of the criminals hanging there abused him. 'Are you not the Christ?' he said. 'Save yourself and save us as well.' But the other spoke up and rebuked him. 'Have you no fear of God at all?' he said. 'You got the same sentence as he did, but in our case we deserved it: we are paying for what we did. But this man has done nothing wrong. Jesus,' he said, 'remember me when you come into your kingdom.'

'Indeed, I promise you,' he replied, 'today you will be with me in paradise.'

The Reverend Shepherd went on to speak in more detail about the kind of interaction that that must have occurred between these dirty, blood-streaked individuals as they hung side by side waiting for the relief of death. He spoke particularly about the man who had recognised something special in Jesus. He was a man who, to all intents and purposes, was finished. His life was over, and a wretched useless life it probably had been. Any dreams of last minute reprieve had been shattered by the first of the executioner's nails, as it crunched through bone, sinew and flesh, impaling him to the rough wooden surface of his cross. The dialogue between this fellow and Jesus was very uncomplicated. Presumably, it arose from what each saw in the other as they shared the same kind of physical agony. What did the criminal see in Jesus? Nobody knows for sure, but it was probably some kind of natural authority blended with deep compassion. He obviously looked like someone who, despite his present circumstances, was going somewhere – an in-charge sort of person, a grown-up. He must have known a bit about Jesus already, the conversation shows that; but perhaps he had never looked closely at him before, or believed it was possible to reach the heights of virtue that must surely be required from followers of such an uncompromisingly moral character.

Whatever else he did or did not see, though, one thing is clear. He recognised a sudden, breathtaking opportunity to make everything all right. Morally naked as he was, there was no way of convincing the Galilean that he deserved anything, nor was there time to live-a-better-life for a while in the hope of investing a little in his divine bank account. Perhaps what was happening was that the child in this hardened law-breaker, the part of him that still wanted to believe in something or someone, was yearning for the warmth and comfort that all children must have. In the eyes of the man beside him, he saw an invitation to be loved and wanted, not because of, nor despite, anything, but simply because that is what children need. Jesus' eyes as he looked into the lost and dejected face of his neighbour were full of the love of his father. They were saying, 'I don't care what you've done. I don't care what you are. I don't care what others say about you. I don't even care what you think of yourself. You're coming with me. Don't worry. Everything's going to be all right.'

As I sat at the back of the crowded church, the preacher's words seemed to be meant especially for me. I felt like a child too. The puzzled little boy who had wanted so much to stop his mummy and daddy arguing so that they would be happy together, but had failed, not only at that, but at almost everything else since, wanted to shout out his hurt across the heads of the congregation, through the preacher who seemed a sort of conduit to God, and thence up to heaven itself.

'What about me? I'm lost too! I'm lonely and ragged inside. I've tried and tried, but I just don't know how to be like ordinary people. What about me? Do you love me like you loved that man on the cross? Will you be a father to me, whatever I am and whatever I say and do? Can I safely show you how hurt and wretched I am?'

Would Jesus look at me from the cross with those same loving eyes and say, 'Don't worry, everything's okay. I know all about you, Adrian. It doesn't matter what's happened up to now. I'll look after you. I know you never wanted to be hurtful or sarcastic. I know how much you wanted to do well. I know you're not the person you wanted to be. It doesn't matter – I do understand.'

Suddenly my eyes were full of tears. How I wanted that kind of acceptance, the chance to start again and be real, to relax the constant strain that the maintenance of my artificial personality imposed on me. This man was saying that Jesus offered all these things in the twenty-first century – right now. As I stood for the final hymn, my hands supporting my weight on the pew in front of me, I managed to control the tears, and after the blessing I joined the stream of people flowing down the centre aisle towards the big front doors where the preacher waited to shake hands with people as they left. As I shook hands with Denis Shepherd a few seconds later, I found myself saying quietly, 'Could I see you afterwards? I want to become a Christian ...'

Adapted from *The Growing Pains of Adrian Plass*, published by Zondervan

ADRIAN PLASS is a writer and speaker who has produced over thirty books in the last twenty years. The best known of these is probably *The Sacred Diary of Adrian Plass*, a gentle satire on the modern church, which has sold hundreds of thousands of copies worldwide. Other books include biography, novels, short stories, a fictionalised account of the author's experiences as a residential child care worker, and collections of poems and sketches.

Adrian's latest books include *Jesus Safe Tender and Extreme*, published by Zondervan, *Blind Spots in the Bible*, published by BRF, and most recent of all *Bacon Sandwiches and Salvation* published by Authentic Media. He and Bridget have also collaborated with friends in Canada to produce a CD of his favourite sketches from the last twenty years called *Preaching to the Converted* while *A Touch of Plass*, CTA's documentary video, is now out on DVD.

A bemused Anglican, Adrian lives with his wife and daughter in a small market town near the Sussex South Downs.

Dave Bilbrough
Singer/songwriter and Author

I remember the scene well; it's etched indelibly on my memory. The early days of what became known as the house church movement spawned numerous informal gatherings in homes, halls and all sorts of buildings.

There we were, I the fledging worship leader with itinerant preacher Maurice Smith, due to speak at a gathering in a bungalow in the West of England. On our arrival we were greeted at the door by a sombre looking husband.

'It's great to have you both here,' he said. 'There's loads of people coming for this meeting from all around the area, but my wife has been taken ill with a recurring back problem. Don't worry, we want to go ahead; she will rest up in the back bedroom and will be able to hear what's going on. But I've rung the ambulance and they're coming to take her to the hospital while the meeting is going on.'

'Are you sure we should go ahead?' we asked.

'Yes absolutely!' he replied.

So after some prayer for the lady in question the meeting commenced in the packed living room of the bungalow. Sure enough after 40 minutes of worship the doorbell rang, and two ambulance men came through into the back room to tend to the patient. The room subsided into quietness as we waited for her to be taken on the stretcher to the hospital.

Maurice turned to me and said, 'Dave, as she comes out of the doors and through this waiting crowd, lead us in a faith stirring song that will send her on her way, expectant and triumphant.'

My mind went blank. As the doors opened and she emerged from the room we all stood up, and the only song I could think of was a song called 'Jesus Take Me As I Am, I Can Come No Other Way.'

Inappropriate it may seem, looking back, laughable even, we

all make mistakes and yet the truth of those words has been brought back to me time and time again in my relationship with Jesus – there really is no other way that I can come to him than exactly as I am.

The more I get to know him the more I realise that he is not in the least bit impressed by my vain attempts to put on a religious display to attract his attention. My religious rhetoric and skilful masquerades will never fool him, he wants a relationship with the real me, not the person I think I should be, for it's only then that he can truly begin his work of grace in my life.

The fantastic truth that liberates me is a growing discovery of the unconditional love flowing from the heart of Jesus. I can't earn it and I certainly don't deserve it, but this simple truth still to this day never ceases to amaze and move me.

The Jesus I know can't be limited to a set of rules and a self improvement plan. I may be far from perfect but by his grace he accepts me as I am – it's nothing to do with any success or achievements on my part; it's everything to do with his death on the cross. He releases me from the crippling anxiety of living out other people's expectations, inviting me instead to live confidently in his love. His grace gives me the freedom to be real before God.

It was on a youth weekend that I first heard the claims of Jesus clearly presented to me. It was thought-provoking and it began my quest for truth. But I didn't want to be carried along by the crowd. I wanted an experience that was real. 'God if you are there, give me faith to believe in you,' was my constant prayer. One September night, confounded by the glorious simplicity of it all, I knelt by my bed and asked Jesus to come into my life. A sense of gratitude filled me as Jesus revealed his love and acceptance for someone as insignificant as me. I was overwhelmed with joy.

Today, almost 35 years later, I am aware that many of my initial descriptions of Jesus may now prove inadequate; my understanding through time has broadened to reveal a multitude of different facets to his character. This Jesus, this 'man of sorrows', who started his public ministry at a wedding feast by turning water into wine, has always defied our attempts to put him in our box, but at the core of his heart I know there is grace that invites me to keep coming to him just as I am.

These last few years more implications of his grace have come into focus for me as I've seen how he has a special place in his heart for the oppressed and the overlooked in this world. The Jesus I worship calls me to care for the poor and to lift up the needs of those less fortunate than myself. Surely the experience of touching his grace-filled heart can only increase our compassion for the vast majority of the world who live daily in poverty and deprivation.

A weak and imperfect a follower of Jesus I may be, but daily I come to him in the knowledge that the Jesus I know calls me to make his grace known to this beautiful but fractured world.

DAVE BILBROUGH, a troubadour of grace, carries three decades of experience in the worship arena. *All Hail the Lamb, I am a new creation* and *Abba Father* are among his many compositions that have been sung worldwide by Christians of all denominations. Recent years have seen Dave developing a vision towards integrating musical influences from around the world to create authentic new sounds of worship. Alongside his music he is in regular demand as a seminar speaker on themes related to worship. His ministry brings an emphasis on the grace and faithfulness of God, and uninhibited praise and reconciliation.

There's more about Dave and his work on his website: www.davebilbrough.com

Laura Perver
A deceased friend

At the end of my second year at university I was diagnosed with a serious blood disease. As a result I had to postpone my studies and undergo an intensive regime of treatment.

At first I really could not take it in. I felt my world had just been turned upside down in a matter of days, everything seemed to happen so quickly. After having prayed to God for strength, firstly to help me accept that life was going to be different, and then placing this situation into his hands, I sensed his presence with me. I found comfort in the following scriptures:

> And we know that in all things God works for the good of those who love him, who have been called according to his purpose (Rom 8:28).

> Fear not, for I have redeemed you; I have summoned you by name; you are mine. When you pass through the waters, I will be with you; and when you pass through the rivers, they will not sweep over you. When you walk through the fire, you will not be burned; the flames will not set you ablaze (Is 43:1b-2).

I was continually blessed by the amount of prayer support, cards, gifts and visits from family and friends, and by my wider family too, my church. It was also a great blessing to attend the healing service there on a number of occasions to receive individual prayer.

I had to put my complete trust in God each day, holding him to his promise that he had a plan for my life, of his constant presence with me, and of his power to heal. I also took comfort in his unique characteristics; his control and his sovereignty.

I remember thinking, 'I don't know how anyone would get through this without knowing God.' It was such a frightening experience not knowing for sure what the next day would bring.

Though I do believe that God brought me through this experience for a reason. From it, I feel I have an increased awareness of being a child of God whom he loves very much.

I know that he is always with me in both the joys and the sorrows, and he is faithful to his promises. I believe that God has a plan for my life and that he will be able to use me to help other people who have to go through similar experiences.

I now believe that there is nothing in life I cannot face, as I have a faithful Father in heaven who is always by my side, providing me with blessings and strength for every situation. I also believe that each day is a precious gift from God.

LAURA PERVER graduated from The University of Ulster in the summer of 2000 with a BA degree in geography. She went to be with her Faithful Father on Monday 9 September 2002. She is still sadly missed.

Wendy Alec
Co-founder GOD TV
(An adaptation of an extract from 'Journal of the Unknown Prophet')

As we enter the twenty-first century, there is a cry that would ring out from Jesus Christ of Nazareth, as he who neither slumbers nor sleeps, walks even today through the streets of London and Los Angeles, Beirut and Ballymena, his cheeks wet with tears for a lost and fatherless generation unaware of his presence, knowing nothing of his care.

But still he walks, unseen, and still he weeps. For the Jesus I know is still the one who walks, his hands outstretched to the meek and the lowly. Still he walks, listening out for the cry of the human heart. For where the world has drowned out your cry in its obsessive grasping for success and power and sway, it is to you he comes.

Oh and how long has he sought you, beloved? How many nights has he stood listening, silently waiting in the shadows unseen by you and those that surround you?

For it was the Jesus I know who wept as he heard your soundless scream in the night. It was he who watched as you tried in your brokenness to put back together the fragments of your shattered life.

And so now he comes closer, the fairest of ten thousand. And as he walks out from behind the shadows and you lift up your tear-stained face to him, half blinded by the radiance of his countenance, he reaches out his hand to you to brush away your tears.

And you hear his tender whisper. 'I have sought you all your life. Through all your pain and loneliness, I have sought you. Each time your heart broke with the agony of not belonging, I sought you. Through each rejection, through each hour of despair, I sought you. I was there, loving you, reaching out to you. It was me all along.'

And as your eyelids gently close as you are engulfed in his tender embrace, somewhere in that nether land betwixt sleeping and waking, you recognise that familiar presence and you know that Jesus was there all along, the Jesus you know.

The Jesus I know reaches out his arms to you to draw you apart from the stresses and strains of twenty-first-century living. For he sees your struggles and where, so often in this present church age his people have failed to take up your cause and have passed you over, his hands are outstretched to you, for you are not forgotten by him.

It is no coincidence that this book is in your hands. Maybe it caught your attention on the shelf … maybe you sought it out or perhaps it was a gift from a loved one. But by whichever route it came to be yours, be assured of this: the Father himself, tenderly loves you, the Master has seen into your heart and has known your circumstance and that just for a few moments he would draw you into his presence, into that secret place where his voice is clear amidst the strains and stresses of twenty-first-century living.

The Jesus I know would speak his comfort to your heart, encouragement to a weary soul, refreshing to his faithful servants who labour for him often unseen and unrecognised by the standards of the church at present.

The Jesus I know would draw the hurt and the misunderstood, the oppressed and the struggling. He would whisper to you, 'All is well my child, for your deliverer is here.' He is mighty in your midst. He takes the hand of the one in the wilderness – in the desert place where all seems barren, where his voice is silent – takes your hand and whispers, 'Don't give up my child; yet a little while and my light shall arise on you.'

The Master would take the minister, weary of toil and whisper, 'Well done my faithful one. Your labour for my gospel is not unseen. Your toil is not for nought.' He would take the self-sufficient and with gentle rebuke he would admonish you for putting such stock in your own talent and strength and tenderly he would whisper, 'Apart from me, you are nothing.' And he would draw you close, that you might know that your works are but a shadow in his sight.

And to you, so judged and misunderstood, the Lord would draw you close and whisper, 'Where you have counted to no man, beloved, you are of exceeding more value than rubies to me. Where no man takes you up, Jesus Christ comes with his mighty arm of mercy and compassions. For the Master himself whispers to your heart, 'Dearly beloved, you are not forgotten.'

WENDY ALEC, with her husband Rory are the co-founders of GOD TV, a Christian television station that broadcasts to approximately 200 nations and territories 24 hours a day, claiming a potential viewership of up to half a billion people.

Wendy has written a number of books: *Against All Odds, The Journal of the Unknown Prophet, Chronicles of Brothers trilogy, The Fall of Lucifer, Messiah: The First Judgement*, and *Son of Perdition*.

Adrian Glasspole
National Evangelist with CMJ

❦

The Jesus I know makes no sense without reference to what most Christians term the 'Old Testament.' Jewish people call this body of work *Tanach*, an acronym for *Torah* – Instruction; *Nevi'im* – Prophets; *Ketuvim* – Writings.

Why? Because the Jewish Jesus – *Yeshua Ha Mashiach* – only makes sense when he is fulfilling indications and predictions we only find in the Tanach.

The Jesus with whom I grew up was a really good bloke; he was a miracle-working healer, with a great line in wise sayings. However he was not God, and certainly was not a Messiah.

If we take Jesus out of his total-Bible context, he becomes just that – a great bloke. In his context, he is living proof that the God of Israel keeps his many promises in very precise ways.

The fact that he was born in the city of David – the House of Bread; Bethlehem, *Beit Lechem* – means little if anything outside of its Tanach context. However, when it is remembered that the prophet Micah predicted Messiah's birth in that very town, and that it was David's birthplace, it begins to take on much deeper meaning. When visiting Magi announced their search for 'the one who is King of the Jews' it's clear that they had been reading Micah and Daniel, but that's another story.

The Jesus within his context fulfils the expectations that:

- He would be born in Beit Lechem – Micah 5 verse 2
- He would be born Jewish – Genesis 40 says the sceptre will not depart from Judah until Shiloh comes. Jewish and Christian commentators agree that Shiloh is Messiah.
- He would die Jewish. If a person is born Jewish, then they die Jewish.

There are so many predictions regarding the Messiah, all of which Jesus fulfilled, that there is not space here to list them all.

So, to the Jesus I know personally.

When I was in my 20s my religious identity became gradually more important to me. To cut a long story very short it was my Jewish identity that really grabbed my attention and interest. I became ever more observant, linking eventually with a very strict group. The group is well known within the Jewish Community for its outreach work, concentrating as it does on encouraging Jewish people to become more observant.

The international leader of the group was the Lubavitcher Rebbe, the leader of the Chabad-Lubavitch[1] sect. We were convinced that the Rebbe was Moshiach (Messiah), and our children learned the chorus: 'The Rebbe of Lubavitch is Messiah in our time.' Why was he Messiah? Because through his work and ministry people were brought back to Judaism; through him people were healed; he gave prophecies. He was the 7th Rebbe, with no children to take his mantle after his death, making him the last Rebbe. He was therefore Moshiach. It made sense at the time – to tens of thousands.

A blow came when he had a heart attack. By this time he was in his late 70s. It seemed odd to me that the Messiah would have a heart attack. It was explained that he was suffering for the sins of the Jewish people, thus fulfilling Isaiah 52 and 53. Not long after, he had a stroke, then another heart attack. By 1991 he was a very frail man. I began to question everything I been taught about everything. I questioned whether there was more than one Messiah figure. After all, some believed that there were two Messiahs: one like Joseph who suffered and one like David who ruled. Maybe there was no actual Messiah, just a Messianic hope to look forward to, like a future Golden Age? Maybe there was no God? Maybe ...?

At about that time I began meeting Christians. These were not like the many Christians I had met previously. These people knew their Bibles, and knew the One who had written it.

---

1. *Chabad* is an acronym for the Hebrew words *Chokmah* – Wisdom; *Binah* – Understanding; *Da'at* – Knowledge. These are the pillars of Jewish Mystic thought. Lubavitch is the town in White Russia where the sect originated.

Over time I narrowed the options down to two possible outcomes. Option one: the Rebbe was indeed Messiah. Option two: Jesus of Nazareth was Messiah.

I prayed for the right answer. What I expected, I don't know. What I got was a shock. I was given a vision of a Jewish man, hanging on a cross; above his head was a sign, which read 'Yeshua from Nazareth King of the Jews.'

Question answered!

There followed an extended period of deeper searching. Was I now a Christian, not a Jew? Did this mean that I was no longer obligated to keep Torah commands? After all, Christians don't. Would I have to go to a church on a Sunday, instead of synagogue on a Sabbath? Talking with many people over the last dozen-or-so years frankly hasn't answered many of those issues. This is because those things are for each person to make decisions about, and we don't have a corporate, Communal Messianic Jewish Halakhah.[2]

Yet the Jesus I met took away my guilt at not being able to fulfil the obligations of Torah. He has shown me what service of the heart can really be about. It's not about no longer being bound to live according to Torah, it's about living in a way that pleases the One who made me, and died for me. Is Jesus therefore a Rebbe? One who is a guide for an extended family? Is he a Saviour? One who suffered in the place of others? Is he a God? One who was fully equipped to lay down his life, and then take it up again? The easy answer is 'Yes' to all these and more!

The Jesus I know teaches and shows the way for us to live; the way for us to be.

The Jesus I know is the One who saves us from the effects of our sinful nature – by showing us the way to live.

The Jesus I know is, somehow, God incarnate.

The Jesus I know compels me to tell others, which is why I'm an Evangelist with CMJ.[3]

---

2. *Halakhah* literally means 'the walking'. It refers to the way Jewish should walk with God.
3. The Church's Ministry Among Jewish People; founded in 1809, the world's oldest Jewish Mission.

The Jesus I know cannot be fitted into even a thousand essays of 2000 words, much less my poor attempt.

Can I suggest you ask God, as I did, to show you who Jesus is?

ADRIAN GLASSPOLE is a Messianic Jew from an Orthodox background. He is National Evangelist with CMJ – The Church's Ministry Among Jewish People. A graduate of Trinity College Bristol, he also serves on the Council of the British Messianic Jewish Alliance.

Lorraine Wylie
Author, Biographer and Poet

The apostle John found that words were inadequate to sum up the Jesus he knew. The difficulty was, not that language would fail him, but that the world couldn't contain the necessary books.

With just a thousand words at my disposal, library space will not pose a problem. But neither can they do justice to the Jesus I have come to know. Still, if Christ could take a handful of loaves and a couple of fish and feed thousands, he can use a few simple words to sow the seeds that transform lives.

According to some, Jesus is only available at certain times and in certain venues. Usually it's the church hall on Sunday evening or weeknight meetings. As for prayers, well they must be wrapped in ancient prose and reveal a sound knowledge of scriptural doctrines. If not, they won't go beyond the rafters. Of course, God is undoubtedly present at every Sunday or mid-week service. It only takes two of his people to gather for him to be in their midst. As for the prayer criteria, well the literary content is fine, if communication isn't important.

But the Jesus I know is available twenty four hours a day every day of the year. I do not have to go to search for him because he knows where I live. He is with me from the moment I get up in the morning until I go to bed at night. As the psalmist says, 'He is constantly beside me.'

The Jesus I know doesn't want me to constantly remind him of chapter and verse of his word – he knows it better that I do. Instead he wants my praise, thanksgiving, worship and all the problems that grieve and concern me. Sometimes, the pain is too deep or the worry too overpowering for articulation. It doesn't matter. He is fluent in the language of my heart.

Just like Martha at Bethany, Jesus is willing to listen to even the petty complaints of my humanity. With patience he waits until the magnitude of his power and glory once again overwhelms my senses and gives peace to my soul.

The Jesus I know doesn't always calm life's storm for me. But when he does, and there have been many occasions when I've witnessed his miraculous power, it is always a humbling experience. Sometimes, instead of changing the circumstances, he alters my perspective. The storm never seems so bad when I'm flying above it!

A recent family drama is a good illustration of how the Jesus I know is unique to me. When my husband was rushed to hospital with a serious illness, I was left to break the news to our family. When asked how I coped in the situation, each of our children had a different reply. The eldest tells how I was cool and calm. His brother complains that I rushed him about everywhere while our daughter explains how I needed to be shepherded and protected in such an emergency situation. Ironically, they are all correct. I was definitely cool, pushy and happy to be led. But the reason for each of these different reactions doesn't lie in any schizophrenic trait! My eldest son is inclined to panic and so my tone remained calm. The middle one is so laid back his life is almost horizontal. He needed a good shove to get him moving. My daughter responds by taking charge. Feeling in control allows her to deal with fear. I allowed her to do what helped her most.

No doubt you're wondering what this has to do with the Jesus I know. The Bible says that if we, being flawed and human, know how to give good gifts to our children, how much more does our Father in heaven know what to give us. This anecdote may be a poor illustration of my relationship with the Jesus I know, but at least it illustrates a very important fact. Just as each of my children find a unique facet of my character, we as children of God will experience a very individual relationship with him. He is the same yesterday, today and forever. His love continues to be unchanging and unconditional. It is we who differ. My strengths, fears, gifts, doubts and experiences will not be yours. I will need a different kind of support, encouragement and no doubt challenge than you.

This is the most wonderful thing about the Jesus I know. It is not what I know of him. It is that Jesus knows everything about me. Despite such knowledge, he loved me enough to die for me. How can I not trust him who knows me better than I know myself? His judgements, guidance and blessings are all tailored, specific to my individual needs. Losing sight of this fact not only robs the Lord of his due praise but denies us the freedom to be the unique individual he designed.

LORRAINE WYLIE was born almost half a century ago in the working class streets of West Belfast. At eighteen she found her soul mate and married him at twenty and together contributed three gifted, talented and very individual adults to society's next generation.

She and her family now live in South West France, having moved there some years ago with a view to lower stress levels with a calmer, healthier and more self-sufficient lifestyle. 'But,' she says, 'We didn't grow enough potatoes, the spinach disappeared and the chickens are part of the family!'

Thus she claims to have discovered that there is no such thing as self-sufficiency. 'What a relief! I don't need to depend on my own limitations. God will provide.'

You can find out more about Lorraine and her work by visiting her website: www.lorrainewylie.com

Brian Houston
Singer/songwriter

How do you describe someone you've never met in the flesh?

I guess we all have various pictures of what Jesus is really like. These pictures probably reflect our values and ideals. In that way we probably give away more about who we are than who he is when we attempt to answer this question. Being aware of that, I enter into this project with a little bit of fear and some excitement.

I once heard a speaker come to my brother's church (City Church Belfast). People described him as a mystic. I didn't know what a mystic was then, nor do I still, but this guy somehow radiated the kind of aura that reminded me of Jesus.

He was warm, charming, funny, entertaining, a little danger-ous, certainly subversive in a polite middle class Irish way and he managed to leave me with a desire to follow his ways or at least get a pint of whatever he was drinking. You see he said things that made me think, things that made me smile and things that lifted my burden off and made me wonder what on earth I worried about all these years. He radiated gentleness and he sought to bring healing and wholeness.

He cracked jokes, he told funny stories and he talked about helping people to die with dignity, compassion and peace. His head was in the clouds but his feet were on the ground and his elbow was propped against a bar in Connemara and he seemed to have an effortless enjoyment of the simple pleasures of life.

Things he said offended people. But the people he offended were the people who cried out to be offended. They seemed serious minded and lacked any sense of wonderment or fun. He offended the people who offend me and the ones who I imagine would love to judge me and I guess the ones I'm judging right now. But he wasn't trying to be harsh nor doing things to impress people. He wasn't showing off or trying to be cool, he was just … cool.

He said things that were unexpected, he disregarded religious taboos and he spoke of God in a way that seemed intimate and made me want to rush in and lose myself in his embrace. He made God seem attractive and friendly, someone who knows how to laugh at themselves and who fundamentally understands what it's like to be human. He made God seem real and down to earth and yet hugely wise and vast beyond my wildest imagination.

Now somewhere in the paragraphs above I left that guy behind and began to describe who Jesus is to me. I don't know where the line is and that's the highest compliment I could pay that gentleman whose name escapes me.

There's a song on an Emmylou Harris album that was written by David Olney. The song is 'Jerusalem Tomorrow'. It says so much about the difference between Jesus and the world around him. The difference between ego and servant-hood, the difference between having a 'ministry' and being a bringer of life, hope, compassion and a reason to believe.

You see I've always been attracted to Jesus, but developed the idea that God was his more scary minder with a bad temper and a nit-picking personality eager to find faults and punish me; the one who I really should be careful of. But Jesus said whoever has seen me has seen the Father. So does that mean I don't have to be scared of God because I'm not scared of Jesus? Could it mean that God's had a bad rap all these years? Could it mean that maybe God was so frustrated by being misunderstood that he eventually cracked and said if you want something done right you might as well do it yourself?

Maybe I'm wrong, but to me this is one of the main results of Jesus coming. He came to cut out the middle-man. To stop the religious zealots from distorting the picture so much that no one could find their way into God's love anymore. He came not to punish and judge but to break down the walls of fear and invite in the marginalised, the weak, the lonely, the ugly and those who didn't qualify. He came for the goats so that they could learn how to act like sheep. Those excluded on the grounds of race, sexuality, gender, wealth, nationality and creed. He came to preach good news to the poor and lift off the heavy burdens. To oppose the proud and embrace the humble wherever the proud are and whenever they humble themselves.

The Jesus I know is strong and well read. He knows what's going on and he gets it. He is not easily fooled and he knows where he was the day JFK was shot and when Princess Diana died. He caught Martin Luther King in his arms on a balcony in Memphis and he sat behind Rosa Parks on a bus in Montgomery Alabama

He weeps with the mothers of AIDS victims and the children of drug addicts but he cries with those who are afflicted also. Somehow he manages to be on both sides at once and radiate compassion and mercy.

He ran up the steps of the twin towers with the New York firemen and held their hands as the masonry began to fall. He was in the planes that flew into them and was with the families of the guys who hijacked the planes when they discovered what their children were responsible for.

He's sitting tonight on a hillside overlooking Palestine watching shells burst their devastation on a village where terrified babies and their mothers run for cover as the Children of Israel carry out their retribution for the latest act of Hamas aggression. He's crouching in the ruins of buildings with them as they find the bodies of their loved ones and he's wailing the death prayers that reflect their agony.

He's watched the American tourists walk around taking pictures of the old country. He's heard U2 on RTÉ radio and had the smell of fresh cut grass, slurry and the burning of peat embedded in his hair and clothes. He's completely involved and completely at ease, both at the same time.

The Jesus I know somehow manages to be on both sides at once without choosing one at the expense of the other. He manages to laugh, cry and dance and joke with every expression of human emotion. After all the Jesus I know is Emmanuel, God with us.

BRIAN HOUSTON: I write songs and make records in my bedroom ... I play shows in bars and places of public entertainment ... people come ... sometimes they buy records and DVDs and then I go to the next town and do it again ... some people laugh and some cry ... some do both ... I don't know why ... it seems something touches their souls ... more come the next time I play ... especially in America ... I'm grateful for that ...

Hey this year I even got a song I did in my bedroom on a record with Elvis Presley, Patty Griffin and The Staples Singers that was released by Radio Two and Warner Brothers ... life is sweet when you're in the company of legends ... Thank you!

Visit his website: www.brianhouston.com

Alexander Roger
Bible Teacher and Former Principal of
Faith Mission Bible College

There was a time in my life when I imagined that it must have been so much easier to know and follow Jesus in the days when he was here on earth. What if I had been the little boy whose five loaves and two sardines were miraculously transformed in Christ's hands?

What if I had actually been present that day in the Temple courtyard when he caused such a commotion and turned the place upside down? What if I had been mending my nets and he had called me directly by name? Surely witnessing such power, such authority and such encounter would have made me follow without reserve or delay? Well, not necessarily. When Jesus was here there were thousands who witnessed similar things and it made very little difference to them. There were even large numbers who followed for a while, but when the implications began to hit home, turned back and threw in the towel.

I was only a boy of fourteen when I handed over my life to Jesus Christ and, even though I have never regretted or doubted the reality of what I did, it has been in the outworking of the implications of that boyhood commitment I have come to know Jesus more fully. The Jesus I know is rooted in history. My fascination with him is all the more compelling because I know I am dealing with someone who existed at a given time, and that the events recorded about him were real happenings. When people ask me why I am a Christian I don't begin with a catalogue of all the benefits that have come my way through believing. I begin with the basic fact that Christianity is true. To me the evidence is overwhelming and leaves me with no option but to capitulate to the claims Christ made and the work he achieved. I wish those who so easily reject Christ would at least have the common decency to examine the evidence first. It seems so unscientific and immature to dismiss out of hand someone who has had such an impact on world history. Wasn't it G. K. Chesterton who declared, 'Christianity hasn't been tried and found wanting; it just hasn't been tried'?

There is, however, another side to the coin. I would not like people to think that the Jesus I know is locked into the past, as if he was merely a great religious and historical figure. A phrase used by the New Testament translator J. B. Phillips rings bells with me. He wrote about 'Christ our contemporary'. The Jesus I know is a living reality in my life. Never a day goes by without my talking to him in prayer, reading about him in the Bible or depending on him to get my work done. Paradoxically, of course, by engaging in these very activities my knowledge of him develops even further. I am convinced that it is actually easier to know Jesus now than it would have been in the days of his time on earth. There is a sense in which his earthly life was restricted by time and place. While in Capernaum, he could not also be in Jerusalem. Meeting late at night with Nicodemus, he could not be with the disciples at the same time. Holding a crowd with his spellbinding teaching meant being unable simultaneously to provide one-to-one counselling to an individual in need.

But his resurrection and ascension changed all that. Russell Maltby, the distinguished Methodist theologian, succinctly stated it as Christ becoming 'absent to some men's eyes to become present to all men's hearts'. The Jesus I know gives me his undivided attention, without in any way compromising his concern for the person next to me who is also seeking his help. It is this that demonstrates Jesus as unique, universal and infinitely understanding.

Over forty years ago, when I 'asked Jesus into my heart', I never for one moment imagined it would be the beginning of a relationship with him that would develop, mature and grow in the way that it has. In my childlike simplicity I understood that I was asking him to forgive my sins and guarantee me a place in heaven. I think I also knew I was making an all-or-nothing commitment.

But there is one other thing I want to say. If the historical Jesus who walked this earth 2000 years ago is now physically present in heaven, how is it that I can say that I know him in my life in the here and now? The answer is to be found in the Holy Spirit. When I say that I know Jesus I am also saying something about the Spirit, for it is the Spirit who makes Jesus' presence in my life a reality. The Jesus I know is an indwelling Christ and it is the Holy Spirit who unites me to Jesus in a bond of intimacy far richer than I could ever have experienced had I only known Jesus all those years ago in the Holy Land.

In fact, there is very little evidence in the New Testament for the idea so often expressed in the well-known Christian song, 'and he walks with me and he talks with me'. Strictly speaking that is a knowledge of Jesus belonging more to the days of his flesh. If my knowledge of Jesus consisted only of him being my external companion on the road of life, then I would be missing out on the full-orbed picture of what it means to know Jesus this side of the resurrection. All those wonderfully rich New Testament phrases about 'abiding in Christ', 'Christ in you', 'Christ dwelling in the heart by faith' and 'being in Christ' are meant to be taken at face value. The Holy Spirit is given to every Christian not to compensate for Christ's absence, but to ensure his presence.

The best way for me to summarise what it is to know Jesus, and who this Jesus is that I know, is in the words of Paul at Galatians 2:20: 'I have been crucified with Christ; it is no longer I who live, but Christ who lives in me; and the life I now live in the flesh I live by faith in the Son of God, who loved me and gave himself for me.'

ALEXANDER ROGER, formerly Principal of Faith Mission College and National Adviser in Religion to the Scottish Prison Service, has also held two pastorates in Scotland and England. For five years he was Senior Evangelist at Cliff College, the Methodist centre for evangelism and mission. He has recently returned to parish work as minister of The Middle Church of Scotland in Coatbridge, Scotland as well as exercising a national and international Bible teaching ministry, with a special interest in evangelistic preaching. He lectures in biblical and historical theology.

Martyn Joseph
Singer/songwriter

Now that I sit down to do this I don't know how to start. I have spent almost twenty-five years as a writer of songs and playing them to audiences that have come and gone, changed and grown and continue to be just around the corner.

There have been times when I was sure about this Jesus, and times when I just couldn't find him. The central ideology of the religion he seemed to leave with us has, as far as I'm concerned, been hijacked by too many and thus rendered impotent in its name. That's always been a struggle for me as I suppose I deal with the apologetics of faith. Nevertheless, I'm never far away from 'God bothering', at least, according to critics.

The thing is, I would love to have ten minutes with him. 'Whoa', I hear some say. 'You can spend your life with him brother.' I have tried that and will continue to pursue something along those lines. I know all about the need to read the book and pray, not that I regularly do, though prayer is another subject and reading the Bible can require a lot of discipline. What I mean is an ordinary conversation where he speaks audible words and answers my questions directly. I would only need a few questions. The nice stuff I know about, but I need to ask him about death, suffering, injustice and natural disasters. I want straightforward answers and I think it could all be done in those ten minutes. I know the answers would be brief, concise and I would get it. That would be all I need.

All I need to what? To know that my gut instinct, some call it faith, was right. That I could lay aside the thousand other questions that arise. Then, however, I'm thinking, what would that knowledge make me? I mean, I would be right up there wouldn't I? Some of the reasons that we don't know make a little sense in that regard, but nowhere near enough to ever stop asking.

Ultimately this. That this stuff is my only hope, this instinct, this ... faith. That's it, and if 'he' isn't and if there are no answers at the end, then ... I should never have had children or tried to love anyone too much. That, I guess, means that the name of Jesus is pretty important to me.

MARTYN JOSEPH has been described as Britain's best kept secret. His career as a singer/songwriter spans 25 years with his 30th album, *Evolved*, being released in October 2008. His particular strength is the lyrical narrative of his songs, ranging from contemporary protests against injustice and inhumanity to a musical psalm to the fulfilment and fragilities of love, or a piercing précis of social history.

Voted Best Male Artist at the 2004 BBC Welsh Music Awards and with a string of humanitarian plaudits and awards, he's an impressive guitar player with one of the most powerful voices on the circuit crafting songs with, as the BBC's Bob Harris put it, 'outstanding lyrical intelligence'.

Visit his website: www.martynjoseph.com

Bishop Alan Abernethy
Bishop of Connor

I was fourteen at the time and I would have to confess my motives for being there were dubious. I was properly dressed in jacket, shirt and tie. This was the accepted dress code, but it was worn to impress the people I was really there to see.

It was a Sunday evening and it was the local scene on that particular day of the week. I was attending evening service in my local parish church in East Belfast. There were two of us sitting on one of the back pews. We were surveying the scene.

During what was probably a very dull sermon we were quietly whispering about this and that. Then the heavy hand of the religious law pounced. We were moved to the front row of the church for the remainder of the service.

This well-meaning Christian felt it would teach us a lesson on how we should behave in church. I was amazed at his action, yet even more confused that nobody appeared to think that the punishment was somewhat severe. Maybe the miracle of this scenario is that either of us ever appeared in church again.

As a child, my picture of Jesus was affected by my experience of church. He was distant and remote, and appeared only interested in adults. The people who followed Jesus appeared to like rules and regulations, and it was important to follow these to belong to Jesus. Compassion seemed to be unimportant and a sign of weakness.

This was compounded by my mum's experience of church. For various reasons too difficult to explain in a few words, my parents separated. In essence, my father was a sick man, and a compulsive gambler. My mum, my brother and I moved to live with my grandparents. My grandfather was a quiet man, although my granny made up for him. He lived his faith and talked reluctantly about it to me when I asked him questions.

My parents separated when I was six years old, and one of my reactions to the trauma of it was that I began to steal. I usually stole money from my granny's purse. One particular day I stole a coin before I went to school. When I came home my grandfather came to my bedroom and told me he knew what I had done. He said he was going out of the house for a while, and if I could, I should put the coin back. Thankfully I hadn't yet spent the money. Later that night he came into my bedroom and thanked me for returning the coin to granny's purse. He said he forgave me, and told me that he loved me and hoped that I wouldn't do it again, and to my great relief he promised he wouldn't tell my mum or anyone else what I had done. He was true to his word and took my secret to his grave.

This was a picture of Jesus I could relate to; the love and acceptance, the forgiveness and the affirmation were wonderful. My grandfather did not want me to waste all that I had been given, and he was on my side. For me, this was a modern day version of the forgiving father of Luke chapter fifteen. The emphasis in this parable as I see it is not on either of the sons, but on the amazing grace and forgiveness of the father.

As I reflect on my own story, there's an ironic twist that highlights some of my struggles with religion as I have witnessed it. My mum, who had the misfortune of marrying a sick man, experienced the cold legalism of uncompassionate religion. I had sinned and found the amazing grace of forgiveness and love.

The Jesus I know is the one shown to me by a man who would say that he wasn't religious. The Jesus I witnessed in institutional religion made me feel inadequate and fearful. In fact I probably saw Jesus as irrelevant when I met him in the form of religion that was full of rules and regulations.

The Jesus I know affirms me. He does not put me down. He does not make me feel worthless or forever make me feel that I'm not good enough. I do not have to do certain things to be loved by him. The religiosity of my Northern Irish culture disturbs me. The Jesus presented can sometimes be very angry, demanding a response that appears to be based on fear.

The Jesus I know frees me to be fully human and live life to the full. I will be forever grateful for the kind and gracious faith of a man who, though he may not have been seen as religious, showed me the loveliness of the Jesus I have come to know.

ALAN ABERNETHY was born in East Belfast. He was educated at Grosvenor High School before pursuing theological studies at Queens University Belfast and later at Trinity College Dublin. He served as curate in St Elizabeth's in Dundonald, East Belfast, at Lecale in County Down and latterly in St Columbanus Church, Ballyholme parish in Bangor, Co Down. He was appointed Bishop of Connor early in 2007.

During his time in Lecale, Alan acted as Church of Ireland religious advisor to Downtown Radio, where he also did his fair share of broadcasting.

He is married to his best friend Liz and they have two children, Peter (18) and Ruth (16). He is fanatical about Manchester United, but we'll forgive him for that. He even named his dog Trafford.

Alan's first book, *Fulfilment and Frustration*, was published by The Columba Press in 2002. He is currently working on another publication on the subject of doubt, while conducting further research in the field of clerical training.

Scott Baxter
Director of Abaana

The traffic lights turned red. It was one of the rare times when they were working; the electricity in Kampala was more often off than on. The cars and buses waited. It was the time I hated most in Uganda. As I looked out the window, I could see a crippled man begging by the kerb; his tangled legs were folded under him and with his arms he pulled himself from car to car. He needed no words to convey his message. He just tilted his head and with heart-rending eyes held out his hands. I sat there hoping the lights would turn green before he reached my car.

'Please sir,' a voice came from the opposite direction. I was surprised to see a young child at my window. She almost leaned into the car as she stared around. A mobile phone sat on the dash, some loose coins and a watch. I was making a conscious note that all my signs of wealth were out of her reach. She was no more than 8 years old, her clothes were tattered and her feet bare. Wrapped in rags and tied to her back was a sleeping baby. With one hand holding the baby on her back, the other hand cupped, she reached into the car and asked again, 'Please sir, give me 100' – the equivalent of 3p.

It seemed as if the light would never change to green. A multitude of emotions were bombarding me: guilt, anger, confusion. Giving money would not solve anything, but how could this child beg for something I wouldn't even bend down to pick up if I dropped it. As I looked into the eyes of that child, I realised that when Jesus said, 'Whatever you do, you do it to me!', he was making more than just a statement about how we should react. He was saying, 'I feel what this child feels! I know what this child is going through, and my heart aches as if I were her!'

We have all been there at some point in our lives. We have all walked past with the words of Jesus ringing in our ears as we justified why it wasn't practical to help. The truth is that we're better at making excuses than we are at making sacrifices.

The Jesus I know lived a life that was all about giving. He wasn't interested in building a big house, buying the fastest camels or wearing the latest designer sandals. From a young age he was 'doing his father's will' and at the heart of that was a love for people, and especially people in need. A man with leprosy came to Jesus and begged to be made clean. Jesus had compassion. The word Jesus used suggested that he shared the man's pain; and he healed him. Time and time again Jesus was drawn to people with physical needs, and they were drawn to him.

The Jesus I know cares about each and every one of us. Not just about the major things in our lives; who we marry, what job we do. He cares about how we feel. He cares when we're sad and when we're happy. He cares about the fact that children are dying needlessly across the world today. He cares about the mother whose child has been sold into prostitution to pay off a family debt. He cares about the boy who has lost both his parents to AIDS and is all alone.

Isaiah 58 paints a picture of worship. The people would tear their clothes and fast for days, praying to hear from God. God replied by asking, 'Why do you let the children go hungry on your streets? Why are the naked not clothed? Why do the poor get no help? Start helping these people and then you will hear from me.'

If Jesus were to come back to earth today as a man, I don't believe he would be a tele-evangelist or a member of a large metropolitan church. But he would have a lot to say about some of the things we accept in our churches. We might even get so annoyed that we would call him blasphemous. Maybe ask the authorities to lock him up. We might even call for the death penalty to come back. The Jesus I know would be much more at home walking the slums of Africa, India and South America, or sitting on a Kampala street with a hundred street children at his feet. He would be mourning with people in pain. He would be mixing with the people we would never spend time with. He would be holding hands with people we wouldn't want to touch.

Luke 14 tells us that Jesus was invited for a meal on the

Sabbath in the house of a prominent Pharisee. It was a great honour; usually only people of high standing were invited. However, when Jesus arrived he saw a man suffering from dropsy, he had hugely swollen joints; a man who was out of place. It was a trap set up to see if Jesus would break what the Pharisee interpreted as the law and heal on the Sabbath. Jesus did heal the man and then turned the party on its head. He pointing his finger at the guests and asked, 'Why are you taking the best seats? Someone more important than you might be here. Take the lowest seat and then you can only be elevated.' In other words: stop putting yourself first! Why are you taking what is best for yourself with no consideration for others? Then he turned to the host and said, 'When you throw a party, don't invite your friends who will repay you!' The culture of the day would be similar to a wedding party in which the guests bring gifts. The host would also receive some form of repayment from his rich friends. Instead Jesus suggests, 'Invite the poor, the crippled, the lame, the blind, (like the man you tried to set me up with as a trap) and you will be blessed!'

The heart of Jesus is clear. Stop looking after number one. Stop exalting yourself. Jesus lived his own message. He came to earth and was born in the stench of a farmyard. The creator of the world lived among us and learnt to be a carpenter. He walked for miles to share the gospel when we won't even walk to church if our car breaks down. He washed his friends' feet and gave his 33 years in humility and service.

Many films today are made about the sacrifices people make to help others. John 15:13 says, 'Greater love has no-one than this, that he lay down his life for his friends.' I want to suggest that since Jesus has already died for us, he is not calling us to be martyrs. To die for a cause takes one single act of selflessness. To live for a cause calls us to sacrifice every day. The greatest way for us to 'lay down' our lives for others is not through death, but through life: 'If anyone would come after me, he must deny himself and take up his cross daily and follow me' (Luke 9:23).

The Jesus I know has set a selfless example of how to live a life full of compassion. It involves us laying down all we have each day at the foot of the cross. It involves us letting Jesus use the everyday events in our lives to transform his world.

Looking into the eyes of that street child, I knew I was looking into Jesus' eyes. I believe in that moment I felt a compassion that was beyond what I could naturally understand. My heart ached not just for this child, but the thousands she represents across Africa. It was a calling I could not quieten. It compelled me to a point where I knew I had to do something. It was the start of Abaana's ministry to street children.

SCOTT BAXTER was born on 23 March 1978. He says that at the age of sixteen, God placed a burden on his heart for Africa and people in need. Three years later, after returning from his first trip to Uganda, Scott started Abaana, a charity with the aim to help young people become more involved with impacting children in Africa. During his four years at Queens University studying Maths and Computer Science, Scott managed Abaana part time. After graduating he spent one term at Capernwray Bible School before returning to work full time for Abaana. Scott is married to Fiona who works alongside him in Abaana, and they currently have one son, called Ethan.

Anonymous

•

A young lady, anonymous for reasons that will become clear, made her way to the UK from South-east Asia to tell of her experiences in a distant land where Christians live in poverty and under the constant threat of abduction, torture, imprisonment and death.

She tells of hardships and suffering endured, she cries out for the privilege of owning a Bible or teaching material for the countless thousands in her native land who long to know more about the Saviour, regardless of the danger. She craves the luxury of a bicycle for her pastor so he can travel more easily from village to village, fearlessly spreading the good news of sins forgiven to a hungry people who yearn for freedom from oppressive ancestral spirits. And she tells too of the physical hunger that is the norm for many Christians because of unfair discrimination in their workplace.

Yet she is not begging for money. She asks only for the comfort and encouragement of knowing that her fellow believers are standing with her in prayer. She tells the story of the destruction of her village and her narrow escape; her face and arms bear the scars. This is her story:

Picture the scene; you are in a tiny church building buried deep in the bush. Christians meet here, often at five in the morning because their very lives depend upon keeping a low profile. There are over forty countries in today's world in which to openly express faith in Christ is to sign your own death warrant. It could be Pakistan or North Korea, Myanmar (Burma), Vietnam or China. The pastor suggests that you sing quietly, but such is your love and admiration for the Master that as you begin to praise and worship, the voices of the hundred or so of your brothers and sisters join with yours as your spirits soar into the heavenlies, lost in wonder, love and praise.

Then during a lull in the singing you hear movements outside the flimsy structure that is your cathedral. You hear the snap of twigs as they are broken underfoot. There are people moving outside, there are angry voices, and then the smell of kerosene.

They may be fundamentalist Muslims or militant Hindus, it matters not, for in the early morning light as the terrified group of Christians scramble out of the burning building, the terrorists are waiting with machetes and assault rifles – and she alone escapes with her life as she feigns death under a pile of her friends and family.

This is the reality of life for up to 200 million people in 2009, and the Jesus I know weeps with them. The evil sadism of those who subjected the Christ to a violent death, places him at one with every torture victim in the world.

The young lady tells her story with passion and eloquence, and the church leaders in – it could be Birmingham or Bognor Regis, Liverpool or Lisburn – sympathise. They tell her of God's goodness in their world that has become paralysed by plenty. 'Things are going well here,' they say. 'Soon our building will be extended. God is gracious, we've already got all of the £1 million we need' – and the Jesus I know sees the deep agony in her heart as the lady from somewhere in South-east Asia smiles sweetly and says she's pleased.

One million pounds would pay the salaries of 2,000 pastors in South Sudan for ten years! One million pounds would feed, clothe and educate 1,000 children in Uganda, Ethiopia or Zimbabwe for five years!

'Why?' she sobs deep in her heart. 'Why do they spend fantastic sums creating extravagant buildings to honour the one who says he dwells in a temple not made with hands?' – and the Jesus I know weeps again.

Paula Cummings

Publicist, United Christian Broadcasters.
(formerly Communications and Media, World Vision)

Understanding and caring about world poverty has been a 'slow burn' for me – a gradual realisation that away from my comfortable suburbia, in the poorest of countries, many millions of ordinary people are still forced to live in unimaginable ways. My response today though, is very different to my response of five years ago, when my action was limited to dropping a few coins in the charity collector's tin.

The change of heart started when I went to work for World Vision in 2003 and soon found myself on a trip to Uganda, to meet people who had been affected by HIV and AIDS. I met many people – all of whom had stories that needed to be told, but there is one little girl who will always stick out in my mind. Isabel (not her real name) was about six years old and lived in a remote rural community. Her dad had died from AIDS a few weeks earlier and Isabel's scalp was covered in white blotches, which a translator told me could be a symptom of last-stage AIDS. Whatever the cause, it was clear Isabel was really sick. Her eyes were drawn to the balloons we'd brought for the other kids, but while those kids jumped around excitedly, she sat on a rock and watched dispassionately.

At the back of our truck, I found something that might just interest her: a toy set, made up of plastic 'princess' shoes and a beaded tiara. I knelt down and tried to show her what was in the bag, but she just looked at me sadly, lacking even the energy to put her hand in the bag to see what I was offering. It was as if – at six years old – she'd given up on life.

I thought about friends' little girls back home, full of beans, who would have screamed with excitement at such treasures, but yet here she was, almost lifeless and bled dry of emotion. For a moment, I was infuriated that this little girl had been robbed of everything before she'd even had chance to live and part of me wondered if, somehow, in this tucked-away part of Uganda, even God had forgotten about Isabel too.

In the years to come, I'd meet other children like Isabel and each time, lurked a thought too frightening to think about – how could God let the Isabels of this world suffer so badly? How could he let it happen and do nothing? This thought continued to haunt me over the next year, but I lacked the will to really think it through.

A few years later, I was in Zambia meeting families and communities where food and safe, clean water were in short supply. This time though, there was something uniquely different about them – a level of hope, that despite the huge problems they were facing, the community had an unshakeable trust that God would see them through. One woman told me that she often didn't know where her children's next meal was coming from but when her neighbour died, she immediately offered a home to his three orphaned children. She had no idea how she was going to feed nine children, but for her, she'd taken a step of faith and God wouldn't let her down.

And that's when the penny started to drop – I suddenly realised that I was asking all the wrong questions. The question wasn't what should God be doing about it – but what I should be doing to show love and help to people who need it. Don't get me wrong, I believe God is the author of the spectacular and the miraculous, but he also often works through us to make the impossible possible in someone else's life. These are often the times when I see the Jesus I know working most powerfully.

My Saviour is to be found in the hands of an unpaid nurse who deftly changed the feeding tube of a severely disabled boy in a dirty Armenian orphanage, and in the eyes of Margaret from Zambia who'd contracted HIV after being gang-raped, but had still chosen to forgive.

Closer to home, I hear him in the words of my amazing friend who lost her dad suddenly, but despite the heartbreak, has used his death as an opportunity to share love, life and Jesus with others.

As for what happened to Isabel, sadly, I don't think I will

ever know. I suspect that like countless other children, she too became a victim of AIDS, but for me, while Isabel represents all that is wrong with the world, she's also the reason why we must fight for justice, for hope and for a future for millions just like her.

It makes me think of Job and David and Jeremiah, all men who cried out for justice and longed for a day when wrongs would be made right. It's a cry familiar to many of us, when we view the world around us. We see so much injustice and suffering, and yet a belief that God sees all and is above all is an extraordinary comfort, as millions can testify to.

However, that understanding shouldn't stop us from trying to change the world now. Although I've now moved on from World Vision, to a new role with United Christian Broadcasters (UCB), I'm still sure that it is our job as individuals to give a voice to the voiceless – to act as God's 'hands' to the world around us.

It's when I meet people like Isabel and Margaret and all they represent, that I am reminded of God's faithfulness and that often God works most powerfully when we let him work through us.

PAULA CUMMINGS was born in the UK. Her parents were itinerant pastors in Scotland and San Francisco. She has worked in media and communications for 10 years, starting out at ITV working on the *This Morning,* programme, followed by time spent with Jews for Jesus, the London Institute for Contemporary Christianity and more recently as a press officer with aid agency World Vision.

During her time at World Vision, she travelled across Africa, Asia and Europe with media teams, raising awareness of the effects of extreme poverty on ordinary families. Today she is the publicist for United Christian Broadcasters, the UK's biggest Christian media organisation, which broadcasts across much of England, Wales and Northern Ireland on DAB digital radio, as well as satellite, cable and online.

In her spare time, Paula writes, runs, sings, travels and attempts to cook. More info about UCB can be found at www.ucb-media.co.uk

Gordon McDade
Baptist Pastor

●

I have always been profoundly challenged by the anonymous poem, entitled 'Risk'. It includes these lines:

To love is to risk rejection
To live is to risk dying
To hope is to risk despair
To try is to risk failure
One of the greatest dangers in life is to risk nothing …

These words ring true in the context of displaying authentic faith in the biblical Jesus. The Jesus I know is one who doesn't settle for a comfortable 'churchianity' but provokes us out of our comfort zones and into a lifestyle involving risk. Here are ten reasons why knowing Jesus involves risky living.

He was poor and homeless

In fact, he told one rich young man that his love of money was keeping him from the kingdom. To adopt a simpler lifestyle in an age of obsession with the material is indeed a risk.

He never did have a job

In our society, 'What do you do?' is an important question because it indicates status and can breed superiority. Often our job provides us with identity and worth. The challenge for those of us who would follow Jesus is to find our identity in him and work out our faith in the context of work.

He counted prostitutes and terrorists as friends

Getting a questionable reputation did not seem to concern Jesus. Mary Magdalene was a good friend, while Simon the Zealot, a freedom fighter dedicated to the overthrow of the Romans in Israel, found a welcome among the disciples. It would be a huge risk to build relationships with the sort of people Jesus hung around with.

He clashed with the religious establishment

Constantly, it seems. Often, they were only interested in their own self-righteous agendas and were exposed with clinical precision. Jesus had little time for 'all their boasted pomp and show'. The real risk is in laying a penitent heart before his holy gaze.

He touched the 'unclean'

Lepers found a welcome with Jesus, a woman with an issue of blood experienced his touch. To risk embracing the 'unclean' in our society is to advance the ministry of Jesus.

He loved children

Jesus broke all the cultural rules of his day in welcoming children. He recognised that it was a child-like faith that would best demonstrate kingdom living. In an age when our children seem so vulnerable, we do well to value them and see them as capable of mature faith.

He worked on the Sabbath

People mattered more to Jesus than empty religious observance. The Sabbath was made for man, not man for the Sabbath. Valuing and supporting those who work on a Sunday is a potentially risky yet spiritually rewarding pursuit.

He believed the Bible

He knew God created the world; in fact he was part of that creative process. For him, God the Father had spoken and was to be obeyed. Reading, believing and applying the Bible to our lives is nothing short of risky. 'Love your enemies; Bless those who persecute you; Forgive seventy times seven.' Radical and risky!

He broke down barriers

Jesus displayed unconditional love and acceptance across racial, ethnic, cultural and sexual divides. He loved beyond limits, and to follow his example demands a willingness to take risks.

He was just like his Father

No matter how busy he was, Jesus always found time to commune with the Father and he managed his time accordingly. It was his primary concern to do what the Father did. What a challenge for us.

This is the Jesus I know and would like to know better. But to know him is to pursue a lifestyle that will inevitably mean risk. To quote the anonymous poem once more:

Only a person who risks all that he cannot keep

To gain that which he can never lose ...

Is truly free.'

GORDON MCDADE is married to Pamela and has two children, Hannah, 12, and Matthew, 10. He has been in local church ministry for over twenty years and is passionate about the local church becoming all that God intends her to be. Reading and eating are the things he enjoys most, often at the same time!

Oliver Crilly
Catholic Priest

Fr Patrick Peyton was from Co Mayo, near Ballina. He became famous as the Rosary Priest, whose motto was, 'The family that prays together stays together.' He died in 1992, and RTÉ re-broadcast a lengthy interview with him.

I was parish priest in Melmount, Strabane, at the time, and I listened to the interview with great interest. Patrick Peyton spoke of his early life, and about how he had to emigrate to America when he was about nineteen. He described the 'American Wake' – the farewell party on the night before he sailed for America. At one point his father drew him aside and said he had something important to say to him. 'Patrick,' he said, 'Be faithful to our Lord in America.'

I was touched by the personal witness of Patrick Peyton, not just because I was listening to a person of obvious sincerity and integrity, but because I could hear the resonance of my own Catholic home in South Derry in the 1940s. His father didn't say '*the* Lord', but 'Be faithful to *our* Lord.' In our homes at that time, Jesus was Lord, and the faith was the ultimate priority, but there was nothing abstract or distant about our faith in Jesus. He was a warm presence in our family circle: he was our Lord. We experienced him in the home, where he was acknowledged through the Sacred Heart picture and through the family rosary.

Going to school was an extension of that. School was a small community of faith, and when we became altar servers at Mass we found a more public expression of our faith, but it was still personal – there was a continuity of belonging. I remember our parish priest, Fr McGlynn, his kindness and his devotion. He taught by example, almost by radiation.

When I went to Maynooth to study for the priesthood, there was a whole new horizon. It was in continuity with the faith of family and school, but there was an extraordinary excitement, because just after we arrived in Maynooth a new Pope was elected,

Pope John XXIII, and he called the Second Vatican Council. There was an impressive team of young theologians in Maynooth, people like Enda McDonagh, Kevin McNamara, Denis O'Callaghan, Wilfrid Harrington. Each day, along with the routine course work, they spoke to us enthusiastically about all the discussions that were going on in Rome; we felt as if we had ringside seats at this major event. We were also taught by J. G. McGarry, founder and editor of *The Furrow* magazine, an older man, but a man of culture and vision. The Vatican Council articulated the faith for our time, for our generation. The Jesus I knew became more complex, but not more distant. The compassionate face of Jesus shone through the anxieties of the modern world, like the icon of *The Saviour of Zvenigorod*, damaged in the First World War, but radiant with meaning.

I read the documents of the Second Vatican Council, as they became available, with a sense of re-discovery. Before starting theology in Maynooth, I had done a degree in Celtic Studies. In the Second Vatican Council, I felt a sense of continuity over the centuries with the communal and scriptural character of the early Irish church. That applied to the written word: I had enjoyed the talks and published articles of our professor of Modern Irish, Fr Donnchadh Ó Floinn, highlighting the ethos of what he called the integral Irish tradition. But for me it also involved the visual tradition of the Irish church, and especially the great scripture crosses. The great scripture crosses, like Monasterboice and Clonmacnois, and the Maghera Crucifixion lintel in Co Derry, reflect the themes of the gospel of John: Jesus glorified on the cross, and the birth of the church. These are peopled crucifixion scenes, clearly flowing from a spirituality of communion:

Lurach's plain:
Nazareth,
where the word of God
was conceived and nourished.

Word-inspired artists
expressed in stone
a sculptured spirituality –
extrusion of the Spirit's features –
as the wind's shape
is formed in snow.

A powerful Christ
with lengthened arms
gathers us, holds us:
beloved disciples
sculpted in unity.

The foundation laid in Maynooth was built on gradually over the years. After my ordination for the Derry diocese, and a few years teaching, I was appointed to the Catholic Bishops' commission for communications, which brought me, through Veritas Publications, into contact with the Religious Press Association of Ireland (an inter-church body) and CLÉ, the Irish Book Publishers' Association. These contacts broadened my experience, and were also immensely enjoyable – a vital factor in education for life!

With my closest colleague in Veritas, Seán O Boyle, I benefited enormously from the Irish Book Publishers' Association. Experienced publishers like Michael Gill and Liam Miller of Dolmen Press were totally unselfish in sharing their experience, and even the details of their costings, with us new arrivals. I wouldn't have assumed that there were spiritual lessons to be learned from the world of business, but that is how it turned out.

I was fortunate enough to come into contact with other specifically religious influences during my time in Dublin. There was Marriage Encounter, and the Parish Renewal programme which Fr Johnny Doherty and I were introduced to by Fr Chuck Gallagher SJ. There was the Jesus Caritas Fraternity of Priests, based on the spirituality of Charles de Foucauld, introduced into Ireland by Fr Peter Lemass and Fr Gerry Reynolds, with the help of the Little Sisters of Jesus. And there was the Focolare

Movement, founded by Chiara Lubich and her companions during the Second World War. For Chiara, there were no boundaries in the search for unity. Suffering was not an obstacle. Identifying with Jesus forsaken on the cross was the key to unity.

The spirituality of unity has a particular application to the relationships between the Christian Churches – the whole field of ecumenism. Sometimes through difficult and challenging times, I found myself exploring this field, in the midst of the social and political complexities of what we called the Troubles. While still in Dublin, I became involved in the work of the Irish Commission for Justice and Peace, including the efforts at resolving the Hunger Strikes. After returning to the diocese of Derry, I went on clergy speaking tours to the USA with Margaret Johnston and later with Dr John Dunlop. I worked with Jerome Connolly of the Irish Commission for Justice and Peace, and David Stevens and John Lampen of the Irish Council of Churches, in writing the *Report to the Churches on Northern Ireland Prisons* in 1990.

That report was the occasion for a lesson in ecumenism from an unexpected source. We were given total access to the prisons, including being allowed to interview prisoners in their cells – a far cry from our experience during the 1981 Hunger Strike. I expected that being part of an inter-church group would make me as a Catholic priest more acceptable to the loyalist prisoners, and I think that was the case. What I was not prepared for was that being part of an inter-church group actually made me as a Catholic priest more acceptable to the republican prisoners also. On reflection, I concluded that one of the values of working together on an inter-church basis is that it compels us to leave behind the power-base of our own denomination. Together, we are, and are perceived to be, more inclusive and less inclined to approach issues with a pre-determined agenda.

I found the same during the work of the Independent Review of Parades and Marches. When we met various groups from all sides of the community, after a cautious period of about twenty minutes, everyone opened up with amazing honesty. I think it was because they had realised that Peter North, John Dunlop and I were not representing our own individual interests, or the interests of any section of the community, but that we had a harmony among ourselves and wanted to hear the truth and do our best to find a shared way forward.

John Dunlop symbolises for me the path of inter-church relations and the spirituality of unity. He tells it as it is, with total honesty and a gift for precise analysis. But he speaks and relates from a genuine trust and confidence. We were in Washington DC together when the Framework Documents were launched in 1995. We were there for a religious speaking tour, but we found ourselves the centre of political questioning. I remember saying quite sincerely that if John Dunlop wrote the blueprint for a solution to the Northern Ireland situation, I could sign it without reading it, because I knew that if John wrote the proposals, he would not only look after 'his own people's' interests, but he would go to any lengths to look after my interests as well. To translate that into religious terms, I suppose what I had realised was that the Jesus I know is the same Jesus that John Dunlop knows. There is one Lord, one faith, one baptism.

FR OLIVER CRILLY was born in July 1940. After ordination in June 1965 he was appointed as a teacher in St Patrick's, Maghera. In October 1969 he was seconded to the Catholic Communications Institute in Dublin. In 1982 he returned to the Derry diocese and served in Strabane, Melmount and Ardmore before his present post in Greenlough / Tamlaght O'Crilly – the land of his ancestors.

He was a member of the Irish Commission for Justice and Peace during the Hunger Strikes of 1981. In 1990 he was a joint author of *Northern Ireland's Prisons: a Report to the Churches*. In 1995 he accompanied Dr John Dunlop on a speaking tour in the United States, and in 1996-97 he joined John Dunlop and Peter North, from Oxford, on the Independent Review of Parades and Marches.

He has been a frequent broadcaster in Irish and English. A

collection of *Thought for the Day* scripts was published by Veritas under the title: *Is it About a Bicycle?*

Jon Matthias
Freelance Theologian

•

I was very young when I made a decision that I wanted to follow Jesus. I don't know exactly how old I was, but I must have been about 5 years old. I know that because it was in the house on the edge of the missionary compound in Africa where my Dad worked as a doctor.

I remember sitting on my bed, in the room I shared with my brother. Dad had just been reading the Bible to us – the account of Jesus' resurrection – and I was captivated.

'Wow!' I said. 'It's like magic, isn't it?'

'No,' said Dad. 'It's not magic …' and then in easy-to-follow terms he gave me my first theology lesson, about how God became a human being just like us in every way, except for one crucial difference – he didn't sin.

I can understand why Dad was careful to make the distinction. When we walked through the Gambian bush to the village, we would see charms tied to the fences, or to the crops – magical amulets used to ward off evil spirits. There were many nights when we heard the drums, beaten a particular way to confuse ghosts and demons. There were witchdoctors who placed curses on dangerous bends and then would take the credit for any subsequent road accidents, or who claimed to be able to heal your sick child – in exchange for a chicken, of course.

So I found out then that it wasn't magic, but something far greater.

I've heard enough testimonies as I grew up in church to know that Jesus is many things to many different people. I think it's also true to say that Jesus is many things to the same person. For me, as a child, he was the wise teacher who cared for sick people, just like Daddy was doing in the medical centre. Later, as I grew into a cynical teenager back in the UK, my Jesus was the quasi-Zealot, the pariah of the religious establishment, the revolutionary voice proclaiming the kingdom. Older again, I realised that Jesus was also a contemplative, a worshipper, a man who prayed humbly before God.

I was studying theology at university when I met the Jesus I know now. In a dry lesson on Christian doctrine, taught by a dry-humoured Baptist minister, I discovered the abandoned Jesus, the crucified God, the dying immortal being. Even now, if I'm honest I can't get my head round that. Like a 5-year-old innocently using the only word he knew to explain what he was hearing … it's like magic.

The Jesus I know is much like any human being – different things to different people. He was a leader, a healer, a wise *rabboni*, a master, a lord, a threat, a challenger, a Jewish troublemaker who didn't realise that his friends had sold him out and crucifixion was around the corner. And he was many different things to the people who knew him best. To Peter he was a friend, a master, famously 'the Christ'. To Thomas he was a leader, an impractical dreamer, my Lord and my God. At different times, the Jesus they knew became something quite different to them.

There's a simple reason why. If God has set eternity in the hearts of human beings, then Jesus Christ sets humanity in eternity. It's a difficult concept to grasp, that in this one person, mortality is taken into immortality. It's not the death of God – but death happens within God. Therefore God not only experiences death, but intimately knows the pain of bereavement, and through that action Christ's death takes on an infinite dimension. There are no limits on God, which explains why one death can take the place of many. And yet God took on limits, in the person of Christ, emptying himself of his glory in order to walk among us and make his dwelling here.

In the film *Dogma*, a reforming bishop seeks to reinvent Jesus as the Buddy Christ. It's a comical moment, made painful by the obvious parallels with many images of Jesus in contemporary Christianity. Within Protestant Christianity, particularly within the charismatic stream I grew up in, we have lost that sense of awe that caused the intellectuals among the Church Fathers to speak in reverent and hushed tones of Easter Day. That which we can't comprehend breeds awe. The superstitious among us call it magic. We might have the supernatural, in the form of Holy Spirit *charismata*, but we have lost the deep magic that captivates.

Of course the reason we want a Buddy Christ is because he is easily knowable. He's the Jesus who tells us that were great even when were not, who loves us so much that he doesn't care if were unlovable, who tips us a wink when we sin and makes us jokingly promise not to do it again. I think the director of *Dogma* accurately depicted the humanisation of Jesus by his followers. As if he needed to be made any more human.

The truth is surely the reverse. Jesus the true human being, sinless and walking in unity with God, doesn't need to be made any more human. But we do. We are fallen versions of true humanity, and this is the paradox so neatly summed up centuries ago. He has become a man, so that men and women could become like God. When we turn him into one of us, we don't make him more human, we just admit how far from humanity we have fallen.

And yet, and yet … it was for this fallen world that Jesus died. It was for you and for me. Somehow, in his eternal nature Jesus saw every death, all our sin and took it upon himself, dying once but forever, in his eternal nature, so that the death we are fated for will not be our end.

The Jesus I know is, in a sense, unknowable. I wouldn't have it any other way. Because in this crushingly sane and rational universe, he is, indeed, magic …

JON MATTHIAS became Jon the freelance theologian in 2004 after he set up the website freelance theology. He has subsequently answered theological queries from around the world, including Australia, India, Ireland, the USA and Zimbabwe. Jon holds a Bachelor of Divinity from Cardiff University, Wales, where he lives with his wife Cathy and works as a staff writer for a national charity. Check him out at: freelancetheology.com

Archbishop Robin Eames
Retired Primate of All Ireland
by Bishop Alan Abernethy

In conversation with Archbishop Robin Eames, it is easy to sense the energy and passion for life that has helped him fulfil his calling. His awareness of Jesus began in his childhood as the son of a clergyman, where the routine of church life dominated. The Jesus he knew as a child was the Jesus who loved him, and the way of Jesus was the path to follow.

During his schooldays there is the honest admission that he was not overly religious, although he says there was never a moment when he did not believe. Doubts were not the issue, just a sense that faith and practice were not always held together easily. His university life and legal studies that followed were to show the great academic ability that would help his faith develop. The Jesus of this period of his life was to be questioned rigorously; the historical details analysed and cross-examined; his analytical, legal mind was being used to question the faith of a child.

The Jesus he knew at this stage of his life was the Jesus of the Sermon on the Mount. The Jesus who was not about religious clichés or hollow sounding phrases, but the Jesus who demanded realism and action; the Jesus who spoke of justice.

Into the stimulation and achievement of academic life came a great opportunity. The young Robin Eames was offered a scholarship to Harvard. But the thrill of this exhilarating moment was shattered by the sudden death of his father. His centre of gravity had been shaken, and it shifted completely. The shock, the grief, the questions and the love of his family meant it was not so clear-cut. Another influence at this critical time was the Church of Ireland chaplain at Queens University Belfast, Edgar Turner. He managed to help relate the Jesus of history to a questioning and analytical mind.

The Jesus of the Sunday School, the Jesus of the 'Thou Shalt Not' was not helpful at this time, and out of his confusion emerged the credible Jesus who was not dishing out pious clichés to unanswered questions, but was offering an alternative way of living. There followed a call to ordination, and so Trinity College Dublin was his destination, not Harvard.

Ordination was to bring many surprises, and none more so than the fact that he was meeting Jesus in so many people. This development of finding Jesus in others became all the more clear because his ministry was spent trying to give support and help to many victims of Ireland's 'Troubles'. It became all the more clear in his role as a bishop. The Jesus he knew encountered people in what appeared to be hell itself, and he made them noble. In their brokenness, the potential of Jesus was present.

These people were not craving for meaning or answers, but for hope that the love of Jesus goes beyond bullets and bombs. The reality was, and is, that there are often no answers to the big question: 'Why?' Trite answers are offensive, yet being with so many hurting people he found Jesus to be present with them, and in them. Somehow in the mystery of suffering, Jesus drew near.

This Jesus did not speak so much of forgiveness and reconciliation, but to the awful loneliness and emptiness that the suffering people felt. He was there with them, palpably. The Jesus who suffered, who was betrayed and crucified, was somehow with the people in their pain. For Archbishop Robin Eames, the Jesus of the crucifixion brings faith to everyday life – and the Jesus of the resurrection gives hope and purpose. He has also come to know the Jesus who is bigger than our mistakes.

This is the Jesus of the second chance. The Jesus that he started out with on his journey as a child has grown older with him and has become even more comfortable. Robin never for a moment doubted the existence of God, but now his faith has moved beyond questioning and leaves him with the wonder of each day. In every experience he finds a Jesus of compassion and understanding

The Jesus he knows is with us always, and that is more than enough because it moves us beyond questions and doubts to worship and awe.

ARCHBISHOP ROBIN EAMES was educated at Belfast Royal Academy, Methodist College Belfast, Queens University Belfast and Trinity College Dublin. He was made a deacon in 1963, rector of Gilnahirk in 1966 and in 1974 was appointed rector of St Mark's in Dundela in east Belfast, formerly C. S. Lewis' family church. In May 1975 at the age of 38 he was appointed Bishop of the cross-border diocese of Derry and Raphoe, and elected archbishop by his fellow bishops in 1986. He is a senior figure in the Anglican Communion worldwide. In 1998 he was appointed to the House of Lords and made an honorary life peer, and he was awarded the Order of Merit (OM) in the 2007 New Year Honours list.

In November 2004, a biography of Robin Eames, *Nobody's Fool* by Alf McCreary, was published.

Andy Flannagan
Singer/songwriter and
Director of the Christian Socialist Movement

Unfortunately the Jesus I know is still smaller than the Jesus I don't yet know.

A few years ago I was on holiday on the north coast of Northern Ireland. It is probably one of my favourite parts of the whole world, but my ability to fully appreciate its crashing waves and jutting headlands was seriously diminished by the fact that on the day before arriving, about £500 had been stolen from my CD stall at a concert. On the day afterwards I don't think it would have made much difference to me whether I was in the slums of Bangladesh or the hanging gardens of Babylon, as the greens were greyed, the sounds were muted and the clouds were darkened. Nothing about my state of mind changed the reality of what lay before me.

The beaches had not shortened, the cliffs had not shrunk, and the sea had not become suddenly polluted. What had changed was my ability to appreciate the reality before me without prejudice. The same applies to our ability to come before the reality of who Jesus is. Yes, we must bring all our frustrations and dilemmas to him, but if we are always preoccupied, as we tend to be, are we truly experiencing *him as he really is*, or a version tainted by our current foibles and mindset? We may miss something of his beauty that is there to be seen. With our current agenda firmly in the forefront of our minds, it is very easy for self-interest to manipulate our image of his character onto the true picture of God.

This is how I know that there is still so much more to know of this Jesus. My pre-occupation with my agenda leaves just enough space to remember, 'What would Jesus do?' in any given situation, but leaves absolutely no room to see or ask the more important question – 'What is Jesus doing?' When I speak to my peers, I realise that this is not just a problem for me. We think 'Jesus thoughts' when we pray about the future and when we say thanks for the past, but we have practically no awareness of Jesus in the 'now'. How can we truly be his co-workers, when we only spot what he has been up to a day or so later, after the dust settles? Right now, ask yourself the question – what is Jesus doing in my life, in this situation, in this town, or in this family right now? Because I can assure you of one thing: he's always doing something. The question is whether or not our preoccupied minds leave us the space to see it.

When I wake up, I am already thinking through my to-do list for the day. That is reality. That is 'sorting things' and calling people, and having meetings. The problem is that often this is my only reality. The great French philosopher Descartes said, 'I think, therefore I am.' In other words, we know that we are real because we can feel ourselves thinking. I am sure that one of the main reasons that as a society we seem to care little for anyone other than ourselves is that to us, everyone else is genuinely less real, as we simply cannot hear their thinking. Can you hear Jesus thinking? Is there space in your head to be filled with thoughts other than your own? Is he slightly less real than reality?

My closest friends are those with whom I don't have to organise an event to have a good time. No excuse is required to be in their company. I can be with them and just be. In these times, I truly begin to know them, as I am investing my brain not in a flurry of activity, but in looking and listening. With these folks, I am able to anticipate what will make them laugh, their bodily reaction to a surprise, or the tone their voice will take in response to provocation. My desire is that I will begin to know my Jesus in the same way. That as with the prophets, I will not only know of his actions and reactions in history, but how he is thinking, acting and reacting right now.

The Jesus I know wants to speak into more situations in our world than we suspect. I think he has an opinion on pretty much everything that we get involved in. A good example of our tunnel vision is in the area of politics. I once received an email from a friend in the USA. It said a very interesting thing. It said, 'Yes, I agree that Bush's foreign policy is questionable, but I still prefer him to Kerry on moral issues.' When did Jesus and morality become separate from foreign policy? This dichotomy is also rampant in the business sector. What would Jesus have to say about this accounting practice, or that marketing strategy? Or do we only let Jesus have his say on our personal spiritual lives?

The Jesus I know causes trouble, and to be honest, we in the West seem to have designed our lives to avoid it at all costs. Jesus called a spade a spade, but in pleasant Christian circles, we'll only talk about the spade to the hoe, the fork, and the trowel. The person with whom we have a grievance is often the last to hear about it. As the proverb says, 'As iron sharpens iron, so one man sharpens another.'

Here are some more things about the Jesus I know. But remember, like you, I haven't seen all of him yet, and that's my fault not his, so any falsehood here is mine.

The Jesus I know would condemn abortion, but also be comforting those who have gone through it.

The Jesus I know would never put a nation's interests above the interests of the kingdom.

The Jesus I know would scream at a world economic system that rapes the developing world.

The Jesus I know would support Liverpool. Oops, I think I just made my point.

This is the Jesus I am still getting to know.

ANDY FLANNAGAN is an Irish singer songwriter who was previously a hospital doctor, but he claims that his proudest moment as an Irishman was captaining England's Barmy Army during the Ashes in Australia.

His audiences have ranged from MPs at Westminster to Young Offenders' institutions, to skiers in the Alps to Gordon Brown at the Labour Party Conference, and he has recently taken up the post of Director of the Christian Socialist Movement at Westminster. www.thecsm.org.uk.

Many of Andy's songs have been used on BBC TV and radio, and by independent UK TV broadcasters. His second album,

'SON' has made a massive impact. The inevitable conclusion you draw from reading the emails to www.andyflan.com is that the songs on that album cause serious life-change.

There is heart for global justice in Andy's songs that is reflected in their earthy lyrical content. Many of them are used by NGOs such as Tearfund, Christian Aid, Stop the Traffik, Stop Climate Chaos, and Make Poverty History.

Recent live offerings have ranted about climate change, the broken lives of young people in the UK, and the effects of the tsunami of 2004.

Desi Maxwell
Bible Teacher

My preference would be to write this chapter in pencil. Ink is so permanent. Books can sit on shelves for centuries binding thoughts in time. This chapter is anything but definitive. It is not my last word on Jesus. In fact I am only getting to know him.

He may be the same yesterday, today and forever but my thinking about him is in a state of perpetual change and growth. There is nothing static about knowing Jesus. He is not a proposition to be mastered but a person to be known. He is to be related to rather than reasoned about. He is to be worshipped not studied. He invites devotion not definition. He is a person not a principle. He walked on the earth rather than being beamed to earth. Watching him stand at the door of the church in ancient Philadelphia we see he prefers to enter our lives through a door rather than a dogma. He prefers to be found in a community rather than a creed. We cannot embed him on a page, but we can engage with him as a person.

In Jesus we meet cosmic Lord and village workman. Totally at ease with the ordinary, he is nonetheless wholly extraordinary. Promising us his return in consummate glory, he is presently content to come to us by means of his own secret stairway in his Spirit. I want to reflect on two places where Jesus brought my faith in him down to earth, literally.

A few years ago I stood where Jesus didn't jump. Recent archaeological excavations at the Temple Mount in Jerusalem have uncovered the south-western corner of the great complex built by Herod the Great. Visitors can stand there and visualise what would have been the highest point in the ancient city. Probably it was here that Satan had brought Jesus at the height of his temptations. Satan urged him to jump and probably if Jesus had had a spin-doctor he would have encouraged him to grab the headlines in the morning papers. 'Jesus jumps! No bones broken!' However, Jesus did not jump. In refusing to jump he sent out a powerful message. The kingdom that he was bringing would be brought in his way. This kingdom would not come by means of attention-grabbing antics but through obedience, service, rejection, pain and the humiliation of death on a cross. It would come through self-sacrifice, not self-glorification. By his refusal to jump Jesus demonstrated a *modus operandi* that was totally antithetical to normal human thinking. The way he worked, and still works, is radically opposite to the way the world thinks. Jesus never entered a church in his life but he is still telling the church that his business cannot be done in merely human ways. His kingdom does not run on business principles.

The second location is on the shore of the Sea of Galilee. There Jesus could have performed a miracle, but I often wonder if he did. The story of the resurrected Lord standing on the shore of the lake early in the morning is well known (Jn 21). On seeing fishermen draw close to shore, fishless and frustrated, he shouted to them, directing them to throw in their nets on the right side of the boat. The result was an unprecedented catch. This may well have been a miracle and I do stress that I have no intention at all of explaining away the supernatural power of Jesus. With all my mind I believe that he worked miracles. However, while Jesus could and did do the extraordinary, it is not always necessary or wise to preclude the ordinary. He raised a young girl from the dead but asked her parents to get her food. He could feed five thousand but he was happy to accept an invitation to a meal. He could walk on water but he normally used boats.

It is a fact that people standing on the lip of the saucer-like rim around the sea can see fish in the water that someone in a boat on the surface of the lake cannot see. On the one hand, Jesus could have provided a miraculous catch but, on the other hand, he could have been acting like a local villager pointing out the shoal that he could see from his vantage point. His friends on the surface of the lake could not see what he saw but they trusted their friend on the shore and in this incident we see the intensity of the solidarity of the incarnate Lord with his people. What a wonderful expression of the heart of Christmas. In Jesus, God was truly with his people and with them in the course of every-day life. Such was his solidarity with the villagers and such is his identity with us today. As the heavenly high priest, his person is as intimate with us as his work is ultimate for us. In heaven today I have a risen Jesus who sees me when I feel at sea and assures me of his presence in the course of everyday life.

This Jesus never booked a flight on Easyjet nor sent an e-mail, yet he is to be found with his people all over the world today. This village workman who expressed such solidarity with his folk is also cosmic Lord who transcends space and time. This Jesus who walked along village streets cannot be tied to traditional routes. This Jesus is truly unique and ultimately self-authenticating. This Jesus is still telling us not to jump every time the tempter comes and is still reaching out in solidarity with those of us who cannot see the big picture.

This Jesus keeps the point of my pencil sharp.

DESI MAXWELL was born in the middle of the last century, and the older he gets the more excited he gets about teaching the Bible. After twenty years at Belfast Bible College, he and his wife Heather launched Xplorations, a teaching ministry modelled on the Emmaus Road. Based in Lisburn, Co Antrim in the north of Ireland, their aim is to excite people about the Jewish roots of our faith and help them meet Jesus in all the scriptures.

You can find out more at www.xplorations.org

Moya Brennan
Singer/songwriter

●

I was brought up within the church – that was very strong in my family. My parents used to bring us to the local chapel every Sunday. That early formation was really important, because when I had lost my way in later life, I at least knew who to turn to.

So there I was, singing in the famous Clannad band, with people going on about my haunting, angel-like voice, and thinking I was as happy in real life as I pretended to be on stage. But inside, I was empty. Inside, I was missing so much! I had experienced the trauma of an abortion, with all the guilt and bitter regret that it brought. I was famous, but I was so lonely. I was travelling all over the world, performing to packed audiences – you're so far from home, you're there by yourself. For a while drink and drugs were a part of my life.

My singing gave expression to a deep sense of yearning, of wanting something – a friendship – someone to lean on. I asked God to forgive my past sins and give me inner peace. And God answered me. Coming to know him in a personal way was a very gradual thing for me, so much so that at one stage, after hearing some dramatic testimonies about how others had come to believe in him, I thought I couldn't really call myself a Christian. But God brought me in slowly yet very surely, and I'm still growing strong with the knowledge that he's there, just building up my relationship with him.

My life is so different now with the Jesus I know. I'm just so happy. I feel so blessed. I can manage anything. You know, when God is in your life, nothing is impossible. Having a relationship with him is so amazing. You get up in the morning and you know that you're not alone. The big thing for me is to try to involve him in everything I do. It can be a lonely place being on the road, living out of a suitcase – but when you've got 'The Best' with you, you can handle anything! As I wrote in one of my songs, there's such great hope out there; a banner of hope when you come to know Jesus and begin to follow his word, when God becomes your God and gently calls you into a new way.

MOYA BRENNAN, 56, grew up as the eldest of a musical family in Gweedore, Co Donegal and is the singer with the Irish group, Clannad. With a successful solo career besides her work with Clannad, she has often taken the opportunity to express her Christian faith through her songs.

She is an active supporter of Teen Challenge Ireland and is the Goodwill Ambassador for the Christian Blind Mission for whom she travels internationally.

She and her family – husband, Tim, and children, Aisling and Paul – live in South Dublin. They are members of a city centre church in Dublin where they are involved in the worship ministry.

Alf McCreary
Journalist, author, biographer

Any journalist who admits to having a religious faith is liable to be stereo-typed as 'born-again,' 'good-living' or just plain 'naïve'. I would not claim to be any of these, but I do have a faith which seems to be under increasing attack from the secular world.

So to define *The Jesus I Know* is not easy, especially as I tend to refer to Christ, the divine, rather than Jesus, the man. However, don't let us become bogged down in theology. The 'Jesus Christ' I know is inspiring, comforting and often annoying – particularly when conscience starts to gnaw at my inner being. To complicate matters, my image of Jesus Christ changes with experience.

No doubt the description of 'Gentle Jesus, meek and mild' was sufficient for my childhood days, but I have moved on from this, even if many modern choruses and hymns have not. Sadly, and God forbid, many church people call them 'songs' as if referring to 'hymns' might put people off. In fact the church is in danger of losing even more people, or failing to attract others, by watering down its challenge to a kind of cosy appeal to those who don't want to mix their Christianity with the real world.

I am awed by the divinity of Christ but one quality often overlooked is that of raw courage. Christ had enormous courage in facing down the critics and the state authorities of his day. He also had courage in spelling out home truths about the world and its people, and nowhere better than in the story of the woman (and the man, who is rarely mentioned), who were caught committing adultery. Christ's response is one of the most beautiful and yet practical stories in all of literature.

In my career as a writer and journalist, I have seen Christ-like courage in many places, situations and people. There is great courage among those who are helping, and are being helped, in the developing world. There has been, and still is, enormous courage being shown in Northern Ireland and elsewhere by people doing their best in some of the worst situations.

This quality was shown in spades by three of my Christian heroes: Rev Dr Ray Davey, who founded Corrymeela long before the word 'ecumenist' had been invented; and Senator Gordon Wilson and his wife Joan from Enniskillen who faced the loss of their daughter Marie in an IRA bomb and their son Peter in a car accident, with a strong Christian faith and immense courage.

It also takes courage to proclaim a religious faith in an age when secularism and materialism are threatening the very souls of modern man and woman. Some people, unfortunately, proclaim their Christianity in a narrow, jargon-filled way, which puts many others off.

However, the people who have impressed me most have been those who did not preach sermons as such, but whose quiet courage in the most difficult of circumstances was a sermon in itself. In that sense the most impressive of all was Christ's Sermon on the Mount, because he lived the words which had been spoken.

So forget about the stereo-type of the 'born-again, good living' journalist. Some people are like that, and good luck to them, but others – hopefully myself included – have to retain a professional apartness which allows us to view life not just from within, but also from a distance.

One of my favourite stories is that of the secular American who held up a US dollar bill and pointed to the inscription on the back which read 'In God We Trust' – but he added, 'From all others I prefer cash.'

That perhaps sums up the attitude of the experienced journalist who has seen much of the world. It is important to keep an eye on the secular, but also to have the courage to open oneself to the challenge and the comfort of the essential message of Christ Jesus, which is basically this: 'Trust in me and have the courage to follow me into the unknown of every day and of the realms of the eternal.' That kind of courage is sometimes hard to muster, but it does make a difference.

ALF MCCREARY is an author and award-winning journalist who is Religion Correspondent for the *Belfast Telegraph*. His long list of books includes the acclaimed biographies of Lord Eames and Gordon Wilson, and also *The Story of Corrymeela*.

Conrad Gempf
Author and Lecturer

I know Jesus. Mostly, I know him from the back, as I'm struggling to take my place behind him. Problem is, I'm carrying so much stuff, it's hard to keep up.

And he walks fast.

Plus I seem to have tied my two shoelaces together so I'm kinda shuffling along and feel like I'm going to fall over any minute. And I don't like to complain, but do I really have to bring this cross along?

But yeah, I know him. I know him in the way that he slows down for me.

I know him when I catch a glimpse of those holes in his hands and side – I recognise them. I wince and my palms itch and I feel like a bag of water and blood; sloshing organs and intestines precariously balanced on two sticks of legs. I know who gave him those holes. I know the assassin; his shoes are tied together too, and he shuffles just like me. Or is it that I shuffle just like him?

But I know Jesus' voice. And if I would just make the effort to stay a little closer, I might be able to make out the words better; I do try to keep my iPod volume down. Yeah, I know that voice and the way that when he calls my name it puts a lump in my throat – all that love and warning and disappointment and encouragement all at once. And I fumble for the iPod, not sure whether to turn it off or up.

On the weekends, he shows up at the meeting place, but there's other people there, too. Sometimes I think I see his face in them. I know him there, in the way he's patient while we sing to make ourselves feel better and then he's thoughtful and nodding when we finally get around to talking to him together and if we get around to listening.

And then, closest of all, I know him when his body is broken for me. In that split second after the priest's thumb leaves it and before I close my hand around it when only its substantiveness and gravity holds it there, waiting for me. Broken for me! I know him in the Garden then. And I know him on the Cross when his blood is poured out for us into a goblet and into our mouths. Shed for us! And I say 'amen' and he burns and glows all the way down into my bloodstream till he gets pumped through me, becoming how I live, how I breathe, how I bleed.

Oh, yes; I know him. And if you catch me at just the right time, you can see my living, breathing and bleeding becoming more like him ... as I keep shuffling along behind the Jesus I know and, better still, knows me.

CONRAD GEMPF is a lecturer in New Testament Studies at London School of Theology. He is the author of two books on Jesus: *Mealtime Habits of the Messiah* and *Jesus Asked*, as well as articles in journals and reference works such as *The Dictionary of Paul and his Letters*. He also worked as a consultant with Rob Lacey on *The Liberator*, with the NIV Translation Committee on the TNIV and with artist/author Siku on the *Manga Bible* and *Manga Jesus*.

Nicki Rogers
Singer/songwriter

I happen to be writing this piece on Easter Sunday. Probably a poignant time to consider and ponder *The Jesus I Know*. I've heard several conversations over the last week about the Mel Gibson film *The Passion*. The film is a portrayal of the life and death of Jesus, and has received such mixed response. So diverse have been the conversations of my friends that it became clear to me that we each have an understanding and need of Jesus which cannot be portrayed accurately or summed up in one man's film.

So what would my film portray? To begin with I may change the title to *Grace*.

Where or who would I be, if I didn't first and foremost see Jesus as the ultimate grace? Undeserved favour. There's a story in Matthew: Jesus walks into a scene where a young woman is about to be stoned because she was caught in the act of adultery. He turns to the vultures surrounding her and asks the person who is without sin to throw the first stone. Then, he bends and writes in the sand. We tend to skip this part!

What was he writing? It was once suggested to me that he may have looked at each of the Pharisees, eager to throw the first stone, and then drawn a symbol or word which carefully and without public humiliation, revealed the secret horrors of their thought or private life.

The Jesus I know is this Jesus. The Jesus who covers us over and protects us from justified shame.

I could try to recount stories of vast healings and beautiful moments, but the Jesus I am in love with is the Jesus who moves in far less glamorous ways. He is allowed to be in the lives of the broken, the ones struggling in the mess, wrestling and battling. Barred, the ones who would be kept out of the Holy Places by the religious. The Jesus I see, the one who breaks my heart, is the Jesus who lives and moves where I tell him he can't.

He gives peace in the turmoil, joy to the grievous, a way out to those of us who find a way to get well and truly lost in the first place, and the second and third place.

I meet this Jesus all of the time. Sometimes I go to church to find him, and he is there, but most times I meet him where I didn't expect to see him.

When I take communion this Easter Sunday, I commune with one who suffered the very worst so that the very worst can be free. I know the power of Jesus and see it displayed in constant acts of humility and love.

The Jesus I know rolls his sleeves up and says, 'I'll see you in there. There's a woman about to be stoned, a man about to deny me, a demon-possessed murderer, and, oh yes, a well turned out preacher, all dependant on exactly the same thing – Grace.'

NICKI ROGERS is a singer and songwriter based in London. She has a wealth of musical and performance experience, as well as quite a life story, something which is evident in both her writing and her performances.

Music has always been the central feature in her life. She learned piano at a very young age, and found a flare for writing and composing away from the restrictions of music theory! Inspired to perform throughout her school and college days, Nicki went on to take music, dance and drama as a career path. This provided her with a strong building block in the arts and ultimately led her to join successful Pop/R&B girl-band ShineMK at the age of nineteen.

She was offered a solo record deal by Alliance Music which gave her the opportunity to be true to her own musical taste and showcase her writing abilities.

It's impossible to listen to Nicki's music and not be moved; everything she performs comes from a place of passionate realism.

Visit her website: www.nickirogers.com

Nick Cole
Media and communications: OMF International

Jesus the Visionary leader

'Put out into deep water, and let down the nets for a catch.'[1] It was one thing for Peter to let Jesus be Lord over his mother-in-law's illness,[2] but quite another to allow him to take charge of his full-time profession.

The Jesus I love knowing is this provocative leader who tells an expert fisherman to fish in the most unlikely place at the most unlikely time. A night's unsuccessful fishing had already shown there were no fish in that part of the lake. And shoals of fish don't come to the surface in broad daylight. 'But because you say so, I will let down the nets,'[3] says Peter reflecting a fisherman's doubt, but a fledgling disciple's obedience.

If like me you live in an affluent country where Christians are not overtly persecuted, a challenge from Jesus 'to put out into deep water' doesn't seem to come along very often. Or rather our comfort makes us such poor listeners that it's got to be an obvious challenge to get our attention. Like the time my Dad and I needed to raise £100,000 during the Christmas holidays to keep production going on a hovercraft for mission and development work on the jungle rivers of Nicaragua. In mid-December the Department for International Development turned down our funding application and the hovercraft manufacturers said we must send more cash by New Year or they'd have to offer our part-built craft to someone else.

Frustrated and full of doubt, it felt foolish, not exciting, to keep following what we'd thought for several years was Jesus' direction to serve the poor in Nicaragua. We prayed for the funds, but hesitantly.

We were enjoying the Boxing Day football on the radio when

1. Luke 5:4
2. Luke 4:38
3. Luke 5:5

the phone rang. One of our team members told us a banker friend of his had been asking about our hovercraft project. Three days later this banker offered to loan £90,000 interest-free immediately. When I excitedly phoned the news through to the hovercraft salesman, his wife, a Christian answered the phone. I'll never forget her matter-of-fact reply: 'Of course, what do you expect? Our God answers prayer.'

The Jesus I love knowing is this risk-taking pioneer, who blows away my small ambitions. He doesn't let me tick over. He challenges me to change, and dares me to let him change others through me; scary, but exhilarating.

Jesus the Inspirational teacher

'… beginning with Moses and all the Prophets, he explained to them what was said in all the scriptures concerning himself.'[4] I have caught hazy glimpses of what it must have been like that day on the road to Emmaus, when I've listened to some of the most gifted Bible teachers Jesus has given his church. In the 1980s as a student I heard Roy Clements preach Sunday by Sunday. Occasionally an insight or connection across scriptures or between the Bible and my contemporary experience would be unusually rich. Simultaneously my mind was thrillingly stretched, my soul joyfully awed, even as my will was powerfully humbled by biblical truth.

I love the Jesus who takes me deeper and deeper into his Father's character and purposes through the teaching of his word; the faith-boosting coherence and 'simplicity on the other side of complexity' (as C. S. Lewis puts it.) At times the literary brilliance and unexpected connections of the Bible are breathtaking. In those moments I feel I'll never doubt its author again.

Whose Jesus?

The poet and pastor, George Herbert described the folly of us trying to praise God adequately. Man is:

---

4. Luke 24:27

A lump of flesh without a foot or wing
To raise him to a glimpse of blisse:
A sick toss'd vessel, dashing on each thing;
Nay, his own shelf:
My God, I mean my self.[5]

Painting our own portrait of Jesus is not only foolish but risks idolatry, warns Herbert. For we tend to plug into those features of Christ that are compatible with the way we're wired. I create a Jesus I like because he's like 'my self' (albeit a sin-free version). But there's also a Jesus I need to know because he's not like me. And by definition I need other people to show me that Jesus.

Selfless carer

My sister showed me the Jesus I need to know by spending hours visiting lonely elderly women in Tower Hamlets. Her ministry was non-strategic and had little obvious significance beyond the one cared for. She also befriended the homeless of Waterloo's 'Cardboard City'. At Christmas time she re-labelled the clothing parcels from 'Woman Size 12' to 'Lizzie', who burst into tears when she received it. 'I've never had a gift with my name on it before,' she told my sister.

Filled with compassion, Jesus reached out his hand and touched the man. 'I am willing,' he said. 'Be clean.'[6] When I read Jesus' encounter with this leper from my professional perspective, working in PR and event management, I seriously question why Jesus bothered to heal this man. Jesus would have foreknown that the leper would disobey his instruction not to tell anyone about the healing and as a result of his blagging, 'Jesus could no longer enter a town openly but stayed outside in lonely places.'[7] The emerging preacher lost access to the strategic centres of population and synagogues from which his message could be disseminated most efficiently. But Jesus let compassion override the smooth running of his preaching tour, showing that

---

5. *Misere*, lines 74-78, from *The Temple*, George Herbert, 1633.
6. Mark 1:41
7. Mark 1:44-45

Christian love is not so much about cosy affection as about costly action. My sister 'got it' years ago.

Patient change agent

By personality, gifting, and I believe, the Lord's calling, I often find myself advocating for change in whatever ministry I am involved in. I have learnt (mainly the hard way) that my vocation is not a licence for wielding a chainsaw in an antiques showroom. The Jesus I need to know here is modelled for me by a pastor and mentor who has consistently accomplished things over the years which most Christians around him said wouldn't work or were impossible. Despite his impressive track record, when he moved to lead a rural church, Pat Goodland was prepared to be patient and allow his deacons 'to chew the cud' like the animals on their farms. He never lost sight of his vision for change but knew he should wait until the people caught on.

Recently Pat sent me an email: 'We commend change as we go out and put ourselves sympathetically inside the doubts of the doubters and the questions of the questioners. It takes time but it usually achieves the goal.'

Jesus said to the disciples, 'I have much more to say to you, more than you can now bear.'[8] Pat too 'got it' years ago.

NICK COLE works in media and communications for OMF International, encouraging UK Christians to get involved in mission among East Asians worldwide.

---

8. John 16:12

Nigel Bovey
Editor of The War Cry *and author*

You can tell a man by the company he keeps. In 1979 my wife, Margaret, and I were commissioned and ordained Salvation Army officers. Our first church was in Lisburn, near Belfast. Life in Northern Ireland at that time was ruled by fear and violence.

Within days of arriving in the supposedly quiet backwater we were in attendance at a bombing, serving tea and offering support to the town's fire-fighters. One night I found myself looking down the barrel of a gun as I tried to talk an undercover operative out of committing suicide. (I must have missed that lesson in training college!)

In 1981 we were moved to Northern Ireland's second city – a community so divided the locals couldn't agree whether to call it Derry or Londonderry. Our call was clear: to serve whomsoever, regardless.

Close to the Salvation Army hall was (the Anglican) Derry Cathedral. One of its stained-glass windows celebrates the work of local hymnwriter Cecil Frances Alexander, including 'Once in Royal David's City'. A phrase in this carol defines, for me, the nature of Christian ministry and the person of Jesus. The second verse begins: 'He came down to earth from heaven.' The phrase is 'down to earth'.

Back then, life in 'our beautiful city on the banks of the Foyle' – as one diplomatic local politician put it – could be very down to earth. Basic. Savage. They were the days of paramilitaries. Dirty protests. Hunger strikes. Punishment beatings. Kidnappings. Bombs. Bullets. Tears. Despair.

It was not unusual for me to pronounce the benediction to a Sunday evening service to the accompanying sound of gunfire. One evening a bomb lifted and laid the roof of our church. The next morning I plucked mangled six-inch nails from the ceiling tiles above the reading desk.

I have lifted a wreaking, puking drunk from Craigavon

Bridge in the first moments of Christmas morning and returned him home to his distraught wife, his Christmas bonus long since leaked away.

On my face I have felt the blast of an exploding bomb. Kicked in the face while selling copies of *The War Cry* in a bar. With my fingers made the sign of the cross over bomb victims as they've battled on life support. Suppered on Christmas Eve with a family whose daughter was blown to smithereens a few weeks before. Tip-toed through pee-drenched H-block corridors and talked with terrorists in cells plastered from floor to ceiling with their own excrement.

Why? Because the Jesus I know is a down-to-earth Jesus.

As a Devonshire lad I used to work on farms during the summer holidays. I often seemed to pick the short straw, which was to shovel dung-encrusted, urine-saturated straw from the cattle sheds. Little did I know it was preparation for ministry.

You can't get any more down to earth than being born in a cattle shed. Forget scenes of 'snuggly', 'cosy' and 'cuddly'. Cattle don't hold their bladders and bowels just because the Saviour of the world has gate-crashed their accommodation for the night. Christians rightly marvel at the miracle of the incarnation. But the circumstances of the delivery suite are also pregnant with meaning.

If the 'lowly cattle shed' of 'Once in Royal' means anything it is that there are no circumstances from which Jesus turns away. No human experience from which Jesus distances himself. No person whom Jesus regards as being beyond redemption.

Look at the company he keeps. His hand-picked disciples are not exactly the dream Sunday-school class. They include provincial fishermen, a tax collector and, in Simon the Zealot, a man with militant political tendencies. Simon Peter was impetuous, James and John ('sons of thunder') were ambitious hotheads, Thomas asked awkward questions and then there is Judas.

Jesus parties with 'publicans and sinners' and is criticised for it. He doesn't care. He is not concerned about what people think of him. He wants to make those who think they are nobodies realise that in his eyes – and in the opinion of his Father – they are somebodies.

So he prioritises the kind of people he will spend his limited days with. Lepers. Sick people. Blind people. Crippled people. Deaf people. Demon-possessed people. Dying people. Bereaved families. Occupation soldiers. Collaborators. Foreigners. Women. Children. Criminals. In short, people who were led to believe they are outside God's love – beyond (as it was once said in Ireland) the pale.

For me, one encounter epitomises the Jesus I try to incarnate – the episode of the woman caught in adultery. Can we begin to imagine the embarrassment and naked shame this poor woman is feeling as she is frog-marched before Jesus? Let alone the terror that within a few minutes she could be dead? While the stone-hearted sex police, hands itching to pick up the rocks, look to Jesus for a verdict, Jesus focuses on the woman. She is the centre of his attention. She is the one who counts in his eyes.

The encircled men are indignant. (Is the person who caught her 'in the very act', as the *Good News Bible* indelicately puts it, among them?) Jesus is the only man present who gives the woman dignity. Is this because he's the only man present qualified to pick up the first stone? Instead of hearing the kiss of death from the lips of Jesus, the woman receives his words of life – 'I do not condemn you either. Go, but do not sin again' (John 8:11 *Good News Bible*).

Jesus pulls no punches. But nor is he judgemental. He does not excuse or minimise sin. He pardons the sinner. In place of condemnation he dispenses grace. Instead of blame he shows compassion.

Presented with the most basic of instincts – the most scandalous incident of his ministry (was the musk of stale sex still lingering on the air?) – Jesus does not turn away. Rather he bends down to earth, writes in the ground and speaks the woman free.

This is the down-to-earth Jesus I know and whose company I try to keep.

The Line in the Sand

Eyes meet, a smile grows;
Hearts beat, before she knows
Her heart is lost, her head's not far behind.
His face, gentle touch
Warm breath, it's all too much,
For him a game, for her the kiss of death.

In the very act they catch her,
Where she has no place to hide.
In the very act they snatch her,
Crushed, exposed and petrified.
To the feet of Christ they bring her,
He should now decide her fate.
At the feet of Christ they fling her,
Stones in hand, they stand and wait.

Hot heads and stone hearts.
Face red, world torn apart,
Her name is dirt, her shame's for all to see.
He stoops, while they stand
Heads drooped, and with his hand
He draws a line, his finger points the way.

In the very act they catch her,
Where she has no place to hide.
In the very act they snatch her,
Crushed, exposed and petrified.
And the very fact they flaunt her,
Shows, in fact, that they're to blame.
And the very fact they taunt her,
Shows they share her guilt and shame.

Eyes meet, a smile grows,
Heart beats, before she knows
Crowds melt away and they are left alone.

'Help me!' is her cry.
'Forgiven!' his reply,
And from his lips he gives the kiss of life.

For the line in the sand reads, 'I love you.'
The line in the sand says, 'Forgive.'
The line in the sand tells of saving grace first-hand.
The line in the sand says, 'You live.'
© *The Salvation Army*

MAJOR NIGEL BOVEY is a Salvation Army officer who has ministered in Northern Ireland, Teddington, Liverpool and Worcester. Since 1994 he has worked as a journalist on *The War Cry* and has been its editor since 1999. His work with *The War Cry* has taken him to Bosnia, Israel, the West Bank and Iraq.

Nigel is also an author with four books to his name: *How to Tell a Children's Story* (SP&S, 1990), *The Mercy Seat* (SP&S, 1996), *Christians in the House* (Egon, 1998) and *God, the Big Bang and Bunsen-burning Issues* (Authentic, 2008). He is also a published lyricist and songwriter.

A former teacher of mathematics, economics and sociology, Nigel is passionate about cricket (a qualified coach, umpire and scorer, he still plays a weekly game) but reckons nothing beats enjoying togetherness with his wife and children, Janine and Andrew.

Keith Drury
Minister of Religion

•

As Toodles looks up at the policeman in the film *Peter Pan* he says, 'I've forgotten how to fly.' The policeman replies, 'One does!' Somewhere between fact and fiction, somewhere between childhood and adulthood, people are forgetting how to fly.

Imagine a world where behind every window pane hides a boy, willing you to open the sash, so he might whisk you into the cool night air in playful arcs, allowing you dance betwixt the stars in a Never Never Land of hope where dreams come true.

As children we are taught to believe in Santa, the tooth fairy and any other fantastical imagination we can conjure up and sustain within our playful minds. At Christmas time we are all caught up in that magical world, where the snowman can fly and C. S. Lewis' children enter their own Never Never Land of Narnia, through the rear of a wardrobe.

But as we grow older we are told to set aside our childish ways and to become a man or a woman, and like Toodles, we are left gazing into the sky, appealing to any who might listen, that we have forgotten how to fly. 'One does,' is usually the answer.

'One does' is also a common theme of the church where the ground crew frown on any who seek to soar. Fairy tales belong in the nursery and Cinderella's story has to be false because the shoe manufacturers know only too well the claims that would be received against glass slipper ware, and anyhow, the mice would have nibbled the pumpkin.

And so as I grew up and became a man I put childish ways behind me. I became a clergyman and encouraged others to stand firm in the faith, preferably with two feet firmly rooted and grounded. Doctrine is a good way to ground people. I found myself in a church where doctrine meant everything. We studied hard, we learnt all kinds of theologies. We condemned those who differed. We paid attention to duty, we observed the commandments, we prayed loud and often. We cried onto God and bemoaned the lack of revival, upon which, we characteristically laid the blame at our own doors and then cried out some more, stricken by the guilt and the paralysing depravity that existed within each one of us. Together we had distilled God of any redeeming grace or gentleness that we might fairly expect to find in even the most reprehensible of fellows.

And at the end of it all, the snowman had melted mid air, captain Hook had run Peter through with his sword, and Peter, Edmund, Susan and Lucy were found locked in a wardrobe because carpenters had repaired its back board.

So, when my marriage failed and crashed, I discovered there was no safety net built into the system; those who crash must burn. The seat belts had been slashed and the airbags pierced by the stoically frightening God I had invented in my mind.

Eventually I left the church, after being informed by a member I was not attractive enough to be a pastor, as my jaw bone was lacking in masculinity. For me, the circus had met the zoo and in one great final tent campaign the clowns discovered there was nothing funny about this beast of the church that roared for prey to satisfy its blood lust.

One evening, as I sat, now pastoring another church, I realised that when I most needed to fly I had completely forgotten how, whether flying was an option, or even a question that should be realistically pondered.

The only two words I knew from the church world I had inhabited from birth, regarding this wingless condition were 'one does', but when one does need to fly, 'one does' will not cut the theological mustard.

Here was my problem. If ever there had been a Never Never Land of Narnia to be believed in, one to be discovered through the back of a wardrobe, mine had come flat packed.

Recently, two American institutions have been arguing about which one has the authentic wardrobe from the C. S. Lewis home in Belfast, the one that inspired his chronicles. What neither of these wardrobes is, is flat packed self-assembly from IKEA.

That however is what we have done to Jesus, we have turned him into a flat packed self-assembly item. A Jesus who can be managed, controlled and built according to our dictates. We can even order him in a variety of sizes for those who wish him to be, well, a little less intrusive.

He becomes a narrow and unexciting God. A God we put together while staring at an encrypted set of instructions written by people who have never had any thing more than a fleeting experience of those who speak English as a means of natural communication.

The end result is always a bolt or two left over. We either hammer them into a hole somewhere, or we throw them in the box under the stairs where we keep such odds and ends.

For me, I learnt that my God had been flat packed, and what was most important about him – his beauty, his extravagant love, his willingness to forgive and his desire to help people fly – were the bits I had filed under the stairs in the box marked, 'One does.'

Now God is giving me flying lessons. I have discovered a God who sets us free, a God who does amazing things because he loves to thrill his children. I have discovered a God who knew me infinitely better than I or my family ever knew me. A God who actually knew what he was doing in the middle of the crash of my life. A God who cannot be stopped from blessing, loving and creating magical wonderland stories out of people's lives.

How did I get there? I guess I didn't! Counsellors helped, I exhausted friends by incessant talking and revisiting of the crash site. I made my fair share of mistakes, and then one evening when I could take it no more, I just collapsed under the weight of it all. There was the first clue for recovery from church control. If you want to fly, remove the weights that keep you earth bound; the baggage that others have given you to carry. Their views of us, their summation of our abilities. Let go of your own perceptions of who you are and often you will need to release the guy ropes on who you have been taught God is. It is only there that a Christian can learn to fly again. Don't ever let anyone serve you a Notice of Air Unworthiness. Only God can dispense these and he has guaranteed that we will rise to meet him upon his return. Guess where, that's right, in the air!

KEITH DRURY is a minister of religion with a passion for art, writing and equipping people to share their faith. He is involved in experimental ministries to the Urban City Centre through creative arts and outreach. His starting point is his belief that God is our creator and we are created in his image. Therefore, by exploring our creative side we come to learn more about who God is. Website is www.sidewaysart.com

Mark Simpson
BBC Ireland Correspondent
by Bishop Alan Abernethy

I first met Mark Simpson many years ago when he was a young student youth leader, part of a leadership team that was running a summer scheme in Helen's Bay, Co Down, Ireland. We had, and still have, a shared passion for our beloved football team – we are Manchester United fanatics.

When Mark and I met to put together these thoughts, we spent time reminiscing. The conversation flowed as we caught up on the news of our own lives and the lives of the people we both remembered. Mark spent his childhood in Helen's Bay, an idyllic little village on the shores of Belfast Lough. Religion meant nothing to him, the regular experience of church and Sunday School passed him by. There was nobody dragging him out of bed on Sundays and he found it strange when many of his friends were not available to play football or tennis on Sunday mornings.

One of his first major religious stirrings took place at the 1979 FA Cup Final when he was a young boy. This particular Cup Final has painful memories for me: Arsenal beat Manchester United 3-2. However, Mark was offended on this particular occasion by a T-shirt worn by an Arsenal supporter. On the front of the T-shirt were the words: 'Our Father who art in heaven, thank you for Liam Brady.' He was offended for two reasons, mainly because Liam Brady played for Arsenal, but also, despite his limited exposure to religion, Mark felt it was sacrilegious.

His opinion of Jesus at this stage of his life was that Jesus was for old people as a kind of insurance policy, or for kids who were happy to waste a Sunday morning attending church meetings. He did not see Jesus having any relevance to his life.

But when he was sixteen Jesus took on a new meaning for the young Mark. He attended Scripture Union in school, and Gary, his best friend at the time, influenced him to think about this Jesus. When he and Gary had a sleep-over, he would find his friend reading his Bible before going to sleep, and this presented a challenge to him. The questions for Mark at this stage of his thinking were the usual ones for someone of his age: how was the world made? What was the purpose of it all? And strangely, the Jesus he was beginning to discover made sense of many of his questions. He was beginning to give him purpose and meaning.

He describes his journey with Jesus since as a rollercoaster ride. The Jesus who was unknown to him suddenly became a major part of his life. The Jesus who had lived among us, the Word that had become flesh had become alive for him, and Mark Simpson's life came alive with Jesus at the centre. It was soon after this change in Mark's life that I met him. The Jesus he had come to know brought energy and vitality to his life, young people looked up to him as he radiated a joy that informed his whole demeanour; he was content and at peace. He was a role model for many and exerted a great influence for good, and for the Jesus he had come to know.

Since those early years of faith, Jesus has been his guide and focus. There have been times when the questions have not been matched by answers, and when his faith has struggled, but the Jesus he knows has been with him, shaping everything he seeks to do. The phrase that best sums up his way of viewing his faith is one that he brings to bear on every area of his life: 'What would Jesus do?' It impinges on his work, his family life, his friendships and, even more difficult, sport. He was always very competitive, and still is.

The Jesus that Mark seeks to follow is now someone his children are discovering. He has three daughters: Grace (12), Holly (10) and little Joy (4).

After the Easter services when Grace was just five years old, she was telling her parents what she had learnt about the meaning of Easter. She was telling how Jesus had died on Good Friday and how he had come back to life on Easter Day, and she told the story in a very matter of fact way. However, what startled Mark was that as she was telling about Jesus dying on Good

Friday, she was fingering the centre of her palms alternately as if pointing to the nails. It is moments like these when for him the word becomes flesh again and he finds encouragement in his own walk with Jesus.

The Jesus whom Mark Simpson knows is an example of how to live, the word made flesh. He is also a model of how to live, and he finds it helpful to think of Jesus as someone who has experienced what it is to be human, and to struggle with all that that means in everyday work and life.

MARK SIMPSON is the BBC's Ireland Correspondent. He is one of the few journalists in Northern Ireland who has worked for all three local daily newspapers – the *Belfast Telegraph*, the *Irish News* and the *Newsletter*. In 2000, he was voted Northern Ireland TV Journalist of the Year in the IPR awards and the following year he won the Radio Reporter of the Year award. Mark became a political correspondent at BBC Northern Ireland in January 1998 and he reported on the multi-party negotiations which led to the Good Friday Agreement. He has been part of the team covering the workings of the new Northern Ireland Assembly.

Outside work, he lists his interests as faith, family and football.

Harry Smith
Director: Renewal Centre Rostrevor

I grew up in a home were both of my parents were committed Christians and where as a child, I made a decision to become a Christian. It was a very safe environment, and I attended weekly Children's Meetings and Sunday School, followed by a spiritual diet of Boys' Brigade and Youth Fellowship, whose officers and leaders were all deeply committed Christians.

It was, however, an environment where I didn't really need to prove God for myself. Looking back on it, my God was experientially small even though I theologically believed him to be big, after all he is the almighty, the all-knowing, and the all-present God.

In 1969 I began my career as a nurse in the Royal Victoria Hospital in Belfast. They were challenging days, living and working with the 'Troubles', the hospital being one of the main receiving places for victims of the shootings, bombings etc. Strangely, I was able to handle that, it was extremely fulfilling and rewarding. It was psychiatric nursing that really threw me. I saw problems in life that I never knew existed before. Prior to that I was able to say that God was the answer to all my needs and everyone else's, but around me were people with profound mental, emotional and spiritual needs – I was out of my depth, and I floundered. My God was not big enough and as a result I went through my first major emotional and spiritual crisis.

In the midst of my despair there was a deep cry in my heart to God. This crisis turned out to be a huge turning point as God heard that cry and met with me in a very profound way. A nursing colleague, seeing my plight, invited me to a meeting near the hospital, which a number of other Christians with a medical background attended. During that meeting, as they worshipped together, God's Spirit flooded my whole being – the pain left and a joy and peace overwhelmed me. I also experienced an intimacy in fellowship with him that I had never known before. It is this dynamic of intimacy that I have continued to know through the intervening 35 years.

At a human level I can best relate it to my relationship with my wife Dorothy. When I first met her I didn't tell her everything about my life on our first date – she may not have wanted to see me again! But as we grew in our relationship the deeper our sharing became. We could share our joys, pains, strengths, vulnerabilities, etc. Now after many years of marriage we not only know each other's voice but we have also come to a place of knowing each other's inner voice, enabling us to communicate heart to heart, without words. It's the same with God. In the place of intimate fellowship with him we come to know his voice and his heart. This I have found is the essence, the core ingredient of intercession.

In the book of Hebrews we find Jesus described as our High Priest, ever living to intercede for us before the Father, as one who intimately knows us, identifying with our humanity. What I find remarkable is the fact that he gives us the high calling of being a holy royal priesthood to minister alongside him – standing before God on behalf of people, and before people on behalf of God – the 'go between-ers,' those who stand in the gap. So intercession, for me, has become more than that time in the Sunday morning service when the minister leads us in prayers for the needs of others; it is sharing in the heart of God, following the promptings of the Holy Spirit within our spirits as he intercedes in and through us. This is not a gift for the chosen few, it is an integral part of being a priest.

But it's not always a comfortable experience. In praying for the future church that Jesus was to birth through his death, he felt the pain of division and disunity very acutely: 'I pray ... that all of them may be one, Father, just as you are in me and I am in you ... May they be brought to complete unity to let the world know that you sent me' (John 17: 20-23). He also carried something deep in his heart for Jerusalem, knowing the consequences of his people rejecting him: 'As he approached Jerusalem and saw the city, he wept over it ...' (Luke 19:41).

We also see this identification with God's heart in the apostle Paul. In 2 Corinthians 2:4 we read: 'I wrote to you of our great distress and anguish of heart with tears, not to grieve you but to let you know the depth of love I have for you.' It is also evident in his letter to the church in Galatia, when he writes: 'My dear children, for whom I am again in the pains of childbirth until Christ is formed in you, how I wish I could be with you' (Galatians 4:19, 20). This is not only an insight into his pastoral heart but also into his relationship with Christ, the Head of the church. As part of the body of Christ he identified not only with the Head but also the pain of its members.

There are so many other aspects to knowing Jesus, but this is the one that stands out for me. It's the privilege of sharing with God, the creator of this world, in his pain for our young people caught up in binge drinking, in self-harming, in abortion, in the brokenness of many family units, of a single parent trying to raise a family, of children without dads. To know his heart, to share with him in his intercession makes prayer an amazing redemptive act. It is truly entering into the words of Jesus in the Lord's Prayer: 'May your kingdom come, may your will be done in Siobhan, in Billy, among our young people, in Rostrevor, Lisburn or Birmingham – as it is in heaven.'

HARRY SMITH serves as Director of the Christian Renewal Centre – a House of Prayer for Ireland in Rostrevor, Co Down, in Northern Ireland. He previously served as Prayer Coordinator for Healthcare Christian Fellowship in Europe, living in Holland and travelling throughout Europe teaching on intercessory prayer and establishing prayer schools in the health fields. Harry returned to Ireland with his wife Dorothy and their three children in 1993, to join the leadership team of the Centre alongside Rev Cecil Kerr, the founder of the Renewal Centre, before taking over as Director following Cecil's retirement approximately eight years ago.

The residential community of the Christian Renewal Centre was founded in 1974, at the height of the civil unrest, as a group of Christians drawn together from different churches and countries, to pray and work together for reconciliation through prayer and renewal for the church in Ireland and abroad. The work of reconciliation continues to be an integral part of the foundational ministry of the Centre, as the community now seeks to be 'a house of prayer' for a fresh outpouring of the Holy Spirit, especially in his church and among the young people/adults of Ireland.

Visit the website: www.crc-rostrevor.org

Jack McVicar

Pastor: The Freedom Centre, Preston

Charlie Brown said, 'To know me is to love me.'

The Jesus I love is often not the Jesus I know, and is not the Jesus I knew last week, last month or last year. The Jesus I know has depths to him that are unimaginable, hard to fathom and difficult to discern. The King of kings and Lord of lords is God, and yet he is a servant. He is truer than a brother, and is a husband to his church. He is supernatural, and yet is seen in the natural. He is extraordinary and yet he is in the very ordinary things of life.

Am I alone in thinking that however much I say I know him, however much I say I experience him, however much I say I love him, the truth is, I haven't even begun to scratch the surface of who he is?

Paul the apostle said, 'I want to know Christ and the power of his resurrection.' That was his desire, as it is mine, and yet we can spend our lives searching and not finding, whistling in a wind of desperation. Whistling to keep our spirits up, to give the impression of happiness, contentment and spirituality, and yet knowing nothing of the personal intimacy and knowledge that go beyond mere facts.

Jesus is supernatural – his 'natural' is 'super'! This may be accepted as a fact by most churches, yet not experienced in reality. We operate in the natural, and so often in our churches we are 100% natural, with nothing supernatural happening to confound and convict the unbelievers and the critics. We have gone stale in our worship and teaching, we are lukewarm and we don't know it. We have settled for mediocrity in our lives and in our churches. Perhaps the Jesus I know would want us to be apologising before evangelising. We have not represented him well. I have often not represented him well.

How do I know this? The fact is, for many years I settled for lukewarm mediocrity. The Jesus I knew then is not the Jesus I know now. What changed? I have experienced the supernatural of God.

Desperate times call for desperate measures. The Jesus I know is ruthless. He says, 'Whom I love I will discipline.' He will strip away any branches, any dead wood in my life that are not bearing fruit. In times like these you are desperate for 'gentle Jesus meek and mild', but the Jesus I know is nothing if not ruthless with those whom he loves. I have known the dead wood to be stripped away in my life. I have known the discipline of God, and I have known what it is to cry out for mercy.

I am convinced that God is looking for desperate people. Often the desperate situations in our lives are God's promptings, he is driving us towards spiritual desperation. If my heart's true desire is to be like him, he will hold me to it. If I have cried out for personal revival, he has put it on the agenda. He hears every prayer, he knows every thought, every desire. He will work all things together for good.

The Jesus I know needs to change.

The Jesus I know is not enough.

The Jesus I know is demanding change.

The Jesus I know and have experienced is often far removed from the New Testament Jesus that others knew. I am truly convinced that if we knew the Jesus of the New Testament, and if we were to be filled with the Holy Spirit, and sold out to him as we sometimes claim to be, the world would be in a better condition than it is.

When I look at my city, my nation, I can see that the Jesus I know is not the Jesus the apostles knew. He has not changed, but I do not have their hunger. I know nothing of their passion and desire, and my nation is an indictment of my faith and my spiritual experience.

I am convinced that the Jesus I know today is not the Jesus I will know next year. He will not change, but I will. Yesterday's faith may have taken care of yesterday's devils, but it will not take care of tomorrow's. I need a new experience and a new revelation of the Jesus I know, and I am dedicated to the pursuit of knowing what seems to be unknowable. Like a lover chasing his desire, I will not be satisfied until I become more like him: supernatural but natural, extraordinary but ordinary.

The Jesus I know wants nothing less.

JACK MCVICAR was born in Ayr, Scotland and is married with three daughters (two married) and two grandchildren. He is co-founder and co-pastor of the Freedom Centre in Preston, with his wife Sue.

He worked for five years as a missionary in the UK with a band called Heartbeat, afterwards building up various business interests. Following a major trial he believes that God supernaturally called them both to begin the vision of the Freedom Centre.

Jack preaches and leads leadership seminars to church leaders and business people, travelling with Sue both home and abroad.

Further details can be found on www.thefreedomcentre.com

Charlie Boyd
Contemporary Christian Mystic

The Jesus I know keeps changing – at least that what it seems like! I guess if the writer of Hebrews is correct, then he doesn't and it's only my perception of him that changes.

As a young man he was my hero and the Saviour portrayed by the evangelical and charismatic subculture that my faith had been birthed in. He bled and died so my sins could be forgiven and I could go to heaven after having 'given hell' to his enemy Satan for the rest of my time on earth. He was a Commander in Chief who saw the whole battlefield from his throne and gave orders to his soldier saints. We could then zap old Lucifer who controlled the enemy territory we were passing through; following this Jesus proved to be hard work!

All good things come to an end however and the day came when I found my relationship with this militaristic Jesus at an end. An abusive church and the sudden death of my first son Joel at five months shocked me out of my addiction to this intense Jesus and his equally intense followers.

The black Bible was locked away in the attic, the spiritual warfare assigned to history and normal life resumed with Jesus taking a back seat for the next 16 years. Prayer to Jesus stopped apart from the odd nod of the head – like when you meet an acquaintance in the street that you wish you hadn't.

I didn't realise it then but Jesus seemed to keep an eye on me even when I wasn't really on speaking terms with him. Life went along swimmingly and I lacked nothing. However in June 2004 he had decided enough was enough and came cascading back into my hum-drum existence. I didn't ask him to, but the new Jesus came crashing in again filling me with the most amazing sense of transcendental love that I had ever experienced. Amazingly our 'strange encounter' had very little to do with organised religion or my free will – he just seemed to gatecrash my party.

The first thing I noticed after my experience was that my anger had gone and a compassion for the underdog had taken up residence somewhere deep inside. I felt a big pain for those who had been hurt and had their lives screwed up by his religion. Out came the Bible again but it read differently – Jesus no longer seemed to be the boss giving orders but the one who suffered with the losers of his day. For three or four weeks I unintentionally woke up during the night and went off to pray or read the Bible for a few hours. Some radical rewiring had gone on inside – there was no other explanation.

The Jesus I know is no longer a warrior but a lover. He seems to hate all religion, even the variety that goes by his name and quotes his words. He doesn't go in for sacrifice – either his own or the self sacrifice that his followers push onto new converts. Indeed sacrifice seems to be a dirty word for Jesus and his Father, contrary to the Christian consensus. He has reconciled the whole world to his Father whether they believe it or not and has exposed the root cause of all human conflict – violence born out of misplaced desire. He has exposed religion as a scape-goating mechanism that looks holy on the outside but stinks with hypocritical violence on the inside – the 'we're in, you're out' variety! His death on a Roman executionary device blows the lie once and for all – we are all God-killers with violence rooted in the deepest depths of our psyches. Religion and politics of all shades have been exposed for what they are – whitewashed tombs – attempts to put a temporary lid on the violence of the human heart.

Jesus isn't into rivalry. He doesn't rival with us so we don't have to prove we are holy – he is not impressed by all our piety – Protestant, Catholic or Orthodox. He ignores sermons, theological lectures, prayer walks, fasts, Gregorian chants, large worship services and all the other religious practices that appear so cutting-edge and godly.

He doesn't even appear to be too interested in our scoring ecclesiastical Brownie points by believing the right things about him.

The Jesus I now believe in doesn't appear to be the kind of God who would start a religion. Who am I left with then?

A Galilean prophet who by exposing skewed human desire revealed the true nature of God and men, one put to death by those trying to hide their violence and finally one raised bodily from the grave by a grieving God. An incarnate message for a broken mankind that cannot be bettered.

Emmanuel indeed!

CHARLIE BOYD is a 53-year-old 'Jesus' thinker. He lives in the old monastic Northern Irish town of Bangor, is married to Carol and has an adult son Josh.

Charlie 'came to faith' in 1967 as an innocent 12-year-old through a boys' Bible class at the beginning of the Northern Irish troubles. Bewildered at how two communities who claimed the label 'Christian' could fight one another, Charlie quickly got involved in interdenominational youth groups that seemed to answer the unity question. While studying mathematics at Queens University Belfast he had an experience of the Holy Spirit which launched him on a pilgrimage through various expressions of the Irish charismatic movement. This eventually resulted in him giving up his teaching post to work full time for a 'Shepherding' Church linked to the American Discipleship Movement. After the death of his infant son Joel he quickly became disillusioned with the practices and beliefs of such movements. A 16 year period of lonely spiritual searching away from organised Christianity followed. In June 2004 Charlie had what he calls a second call and conversion with emphasis on the love of God. He does not align with any institutional 'church' but has a desire to see unity between all those whom he calls 'children of God'. The works of French thinker Rene Girard have had a profound influence on his thoughts regarding why rivalry is so prevalent among God believers.

Deborah Drury
Irish Schoolteacher

When you ask most people today who they think Jesus is, answers will range from 'a great teacher' to 'the Son of God' or even a few 'I don't know's.

To many others Jesus is simply recognisable from popular culture where song-writers have made him into the star of their musical successes – a couple of well-known examples include Depeche Mode's *Personal Jesus* which has been recorded by Johnny Cash and Marilyn Manson, and Bruce Springsteen's *Jesus was an Only Son*. Apparently you can even purchase a Jesus 'action man' now which boasts 'posable arms and gliding action!' I am guessing that the action figure doesn't literally 'glide' through the heavens or walk on water, but isn't it interesting that Jesus is now being mass produced in plastic and metal? The creator of the heavens and earth has become a plaything for anyone over three years old – small pieces limit the market somewhat; we couldn't have Jesus killing anyone. I have just returned from a trip to the USA where T-shirts are readily available with 'Jesus Loves Me' printed on them, but far from being sold in Christian bookstores, these are part of mass market fashion where even television celebrities model the item as part of the endorsement process.

As a minister's daughter growing up in a church where God was viewed as an awesome being, even the very suggestion of Jesus being moulded into plastic and sold in a cardboard box, or sung about by rock stars, would have been viewed as blasphemous and denigrating to an all-holy God. And maybe it is questionable, but this Jesus was only worthy of discussion in church or someone you could talk to using archaic language in sacred prayer – preferably with a 'head covering' and in a skirt you could trip in if you were female. Even wearing a T-shirt displaying a 'Jesus Loves Me' slogan would have been seen as reprehensible if you didn't really understand what that meant. Jesus was as far removed from the culture of everyday living as my aging ten-year-old VW Golf is removed from the sparkling new Audi sports car I test drove yesterday.

Don't misunderstand me, I fully believe that God is an all-powerful God who ought to be treated with reverence and respect, but the Jesus I knew back then meant you were expected to live within a heavenly bubble that had little earthly relevance. The very idea of Jesus being in any way integrated into 'worldly' things was to pollute and dilute the essence of his purity. It therefore followed that Christians needed to stay as far away as possible from non-Christians, disassociating themselves from 'the ungodly'.

If a lady attended church without a head-covering, she was immediately branded 'unsaved' and her name added to the prayer list. If a young person listened to rock or pop music, it was said they were being injected with occult subliminal messages and were likely to rebel against the authority of their parents. For a woman to wear any Max-factor product was to present herself as a seductress that showed she had a Jezebel spirit, indeed one could never follow worldly fashions since you had be distinctive in demure long skirts (without a slit) and loose tops that didn't draw attention to any God-given curves. Even attending the cinema was dangerous, and clubbing was a definite no-no. Associating with non-Christian 'friends' was labelled 'bad company' and homosexuals were excommunicated from the church. In services believers were called to be 'separate' – a peculiar people set apart. Peculiar, yes, I was certainly that!

As a twelve-year-old I remember the sheer terror I encountered when I read the title of my end of term English exam: 'Write about your favourite television programme' – we didn't have a TV – it was too dangerous.

Yet when you consider the Jesus of the New Testament, it is clear that he integrated himself fully into the world of his day. He befriended tax-collectors, prostitutes, outsiders and the diseased. The Pharisees or religious leaders asked the disciples, 'Why does your teacher eat with tax collectors and "sinners"?'

On hearing this, Jesus said, 'It is not the healthy who need a doctor, but the sick' (Matthew 9:10-12 *NIV*).

The Jesus I know today is very different from the Jesus I grew up with. As a minister's wife in a city-centre church, I have come to appreciate the absolute necessity of spending time with those who are not in any way religious. Jesus doesn't want us to live comfortably in our little 'sub-cultures' with our Christian bands and weekends away with cheesy promises of 'food, fellowship and fun' – he wants us be living, vibrant people who are real and clued in to the society he has allowed us to be a part of.

Our church doors are open Monday to Friday for people to wander in and encounter God in a non-threatening and non-confrontational way. A church café has been installed in the basement which provides a place where church members can build friendships and trust before inviting business colleagues, friends or family to one of the many lunchtime services in the sanctuary. A Christian nightclub has been introduced to allow young people to bring unchurched friends to and enjoy an evening without the pressures of alcohol and drug abuse. Businessmen have the opportunity to attend an Economic Forum every month to see how biblical principles can apply to present economic dilemmas. National orchestras have held concerts, and art exhibitions are regularly on display.

In Tolkien's *The Fellowship of the Rings*, Galadriel talks to Frodo about the changes in Middle Earth in this classic line: 'The world has changed. I feel it in the water. I feel it in the earth. I smell it in the air.'

The twenty-first century church needs to be clued in to these changes and rather than alienating and disassociating themselves from non-Christians, they should ensure that they present the gospel in ways that allow them the opportunity to enter a church building without feeling judged. So, rather than present our theological hang-ups to a cynical society, why not present Jesus? And the good news is he is a real person, not a plastic action man in a cardboard box.

DEBORAH DRURY began training in law but switched to English Literature to follow her main passion in life. Now an English teacher, she combines her busy teaching career with assisting her husband in promoting urban mission in Central Belfast, often through innovative and unconventional methods.

Paddy McCafferty
Catholic Priest

Jesus was once asked by the people of Capernaum: 'Master, when did you come here?' (Jn 6:26). As the Incarnate Word, Jesus located himself, geographically and historically, within communities of human beings.

It was in towns, villages and the countryside, as he travelled, preached and lived among people, that he made the Father known in the power of the Holy Spirit.

The place where I first met Jesus was Rathcoole, North Belfast, at that time regarded as the largest housing estate in Europe, where my family lived when I was born. And it was there – and later in Whiteabbey – that I first came to know and love God, in Jesus Christ, through the example of my parents, grandparents, relations, neighbours – Catholic and Protestant – priests, religious sisters and the parish communities of Our Lady, Star of the Sea, Whitehouse and St James, Whiteabbey.

I was drawn to God from a very young age. I quickly developed a love of the Mass and the worship of the church. I became an altar server aged seven. I went to Mass and served Mass almost every day of my childhood and teenage years. The priests I knew as a child were kind and godly men. They inspired me. I wanted to live the kind of life they were living: Fr James Close, Fr Eamon Magee, Fr Eugene McArdle, Fr Hugh Starkey. From a very young age, I felt called to the priesthood.

All of this might sound very safe, pious and nice. But it was not an idyllic childhood. I was sexually abused as a child by a female babysitter and later by a local male neighbour. These experiences occurred when I was aged about four to seven years old and I was profoundly and lastingly traumatised.

A very dark and frightening world was opened up to me. In fact, the world in which I – and countless others grew up – was crazy, violent and perilous. The Northern Ireland 'Troubles' erupted when I was five years old. At age eight, my family were forced to leave our home in Rathcoole by the UDA – a violent paramilitary organisation. We were homeless – going from pillar to post – for the next four years. These sufferings – and much worse – were shared by a multitude of people, Catholic and Protestant, during that entire tragic epoch.

In the midst of all this anxiety and distress, I took refuge in God, in the church and in faith. Later in life, when I began to read the Psalms, I found many beautiful descriptions of God's sheltering and protecting love. For example: 'The Lord is my Rock and fortress, my deliverer is my God … my stronghold, my place of refuge' (Ps 18:2). In the midst of an insane, unpredictable and dangerous world, in God and God's church was consolation and peace.

At age eleven, I went to St Malachy's College, Belfast, which in those days – the mid seventies – was a fearsome place. I was frightened and unhappy. There, I saw a less wholesome side of the priesthood and Catholic life; but I knew the God of my childhood was not like some of those who were supposed to be representing him.

At age eighteen, September 1981, I entered the seminary to study for the priesthood which, I believed, was exactly the right direction for my life to take. Little did I know that further horrific experiences were ahead, of sexual assault by a priest, when I would be home from the seminary on holiday. At that stage of life – although no longer a child technically – I looked very much younger than my years.

The experiences at the hands of this priest had a devastating effect upon me and compounded the injuries already inflicted. I felt helpless and powerless and did not know where to turn for help. I entered a long period of deep darkness and, although I continued to pray, there was no longer any comfort or peace – only depression and chaos.

Nevertheless, I persevered as I was determined to serve God and God's people as a priest. I was ordained on 25 June 1989 and have never doubted God's call since my youngest days. My experiences, however, as a child and young adult, have left me deeply wounded and those wounds need ongoing attention.

My relationship with God the Father, through his Son, Jesus, in the love of the Holy Spirit, has enabled me to keep going through many periods of prolonged and recurrent depression and suffering. As a Catholic priest, at the centre of my life is the daily celebration of the Eucharist, from which I draw strength, hope and courage.

I would not say that faith 'comforts' me as such and, I think, that is the difference between the Jesus to whom I related as a child and Jesus who walks with me now. The change, of course, is on my part for he is 'the same, yesterday, today and forever' (Heb 13:8). My present relationship is very much with the suffering and traumatised Lord, who cried out to his Father: 'Why have you forsaken me?' (Mark 15:34). On the cross, he knew no comfort.

I meditate much on the Christ of Holy Saturday – dead and buried – laid in the dark tomb. Where is the Father and the Holy Spirit? It would seem that all is lost. But we know that is not how it ends. I saw an Icon once, showing God the Father emerging from the tomb with his arms around the torn, bloodied and lifeless body of his Son. The Holy Spirit, in the form of a dove, hovered overhead.

I know that 'the Spirit of him who raised Jesus from the dead is living in us' (Rom 8:11) and that whatever, in life, leaves us feeling battered and bruised – maybe even drained of life – we have the assurance of 'victory through our Lord Jesus Christ' (1 Cor 15:57). The place of trauma becomes the ground where God is encountered and the wounds inflicted can be inroads for grace.

As a child, I had a very 'visual' relationship with God – I could picture everything in my mind: God, heaven, Mary, the angels and saints, etc. That is no longer the case. When I try to imagine God, my mind falls flat. I know from my study of spirituality and theology that this is nothing to be alarmed about – quite the opposite.

I continue to struggle with the issues that have caused me suffering. In so far as pain can be alleviated I seek assistance. I may be wounded but I am definitely walking and doing my best, weak and sinful like every other human being, to love and serve God in God's people.

Whatever happens, I am not turning back – only going forward 'by faith and not by sight' (2 Cor 5:7), shepherded today as an adult, as I was when a boy, by the One who – 'even if I should walk in the valley of the shadow of death' – says to me, 'I am here. For you, Lord, are at my side' (Ps 23:4).

FR PATRICK MCCAFFERTY was born in 1963 and is the eldest of four children. He was educated at Stella Maris Primary School, Rathcoole, St James' Primary School, Whiteabbey and St Malachy's College, Belfast. He studied for the priesthood at St Peter's College, Wexford and St Patrick's College, Maynooth. He was ordained a priest for the diocese of Down and Connor on 25 June 1989, in St Peter's Cathedral, Belfast, by the then bishop of Down and Connor, the Most Rev Cahal B. Daly.

Patrick's first assignment was a brief period in Downpatrick, Co Down – September 1989-February 1990. He was then appointed curate in Nativity, Poleglass, where he served from February 1990-August 1994. He subsequently held positions as curate in Holy Trinity, Belfast (1994-1998), Sacred Heart, Belfast (1998-2002) and St Patrick's, Lisburn, (August 2002-January 2003).

In January 2003, after many years of suffering as a result of sexual abuse in childhood and young adulthood, he sought help and care – with the support of the diocese of Down and Connor – in the USA, and during that period also ministered in the Parish of St Ann, North Oxford, MA.

In September 2004, he was sent by the Bishop of Down and Connor, the Most Rev Patrick Walsh, for post-graduate studies in theology to The Milltown Institute, Dublin and appointed Parish Chaplain in Rathmines, by Archbishop Diarmuid Martin. In October 2006, he was conferred with a Licentiate in Sacred Theology (STL) and is currently pursuing doctoral studies in theology at Milltown, whilst continuing to minister in Rathmines.

James Ryle
Bible Teacher
by Adam Harbinson

The Jesus I know is definitely not religious. He's the best friend you could ever have. He's good company, he's noble and inspiring. He's so good to be around. When we get busy, under pressure, up tight, he draws alongside and says, 'Relax. I want to enjoy your company.' The Jesus I know brings truth, love and power. He is real. He is relevant, and he is significant.

James Ryle, by his own admission, is regarded by some of his contemporaries as being a little 'kookie'. Spend only an hour in his company and you might agree, but scratch the surface and you'll find a man whose relationship is uncommonly personal and real – as it should be. That God should speak to us is the norm, he believes, and to those who would raise an eyebrow, James says, 'What? You've never heard from God?'

26 October 2001 was James' 51st birthday. He was travelling to a men's retreat far from home, and he was having a 'blue' day. He recalls, 'I began to sing, "Create in me a clean heart, O God," and I was crying as I drove along, but when I checked into my hotel they gave me Room 101. That's the number of my home!'

He says he thought God might have something to show him while staying in that room. Walking in, he found a Gideon Bible on the coffee table, lying open at Psalm 51. 'It was my 51st birthday,' James said, 'and as I read down the Psalm there were those words: create in me a clean heart. That was my birthday present from Jesus.'

A few years ago James Ryle travelled from America to conduct a conference in West Presbyterian Church in Bangor, Ireland. 'Everything that could go wrong, had gone wrong,' he wailed. 'The airline had lost my luggage, and with it, all my sermon notes. As I stood in the pulpit on Sunday morning, feeling awful, a shaft of sunlight fell on my back. I could feel its heat, and it was like God's hand on my shoulder, and he was saying, 'It's OK son. I'm here.'

It's not unusual, apparently, to find James out on the golf greens with his bag of clubs – and two golf balls. Does he really play golf with Jesus? 'Yes I do, and why not? He's my best friend!'

To him it's the most natural thing in the world: 'We chat and joke and enjoy each other's company.' James tells of a time when they were playing a par three hole. James went first … and it was a beauty. Straight down the fairway, hit the edge of the green and bounced to within ten feet of the hole.

'That's gonna be a tough one to beat,' he crooned to his invisible but very real friend, and for the second time, this time playing Jesus' shot, he squared up to the ball, 'But I (or he) was trying too hard and I pulled the stroke.' The ball took off, but way in the wrong direction. 'Aw no,' groaned James feeling that he had hit the Lord's ball out of bounds. But the ball hit the top of a fence, bounced back toward the green and ended up just two feet from the flag, closer than James' shot. 'Now that's not fair!'

James believes that golf has a lot to teach us about the Christian life: 'Keep your knees bent and your head down. Keep a firm grip with a good follow-through.'

Kookie? Maybe not, maybe he is a man so secure in himself and in his relationship with his Jesus, his best friend, that he's totally free to be who he wants to be. However, the question that struck me as I left this remarkable man's company was: does he pay two green fees?

JAMES RYLE: Placed in an orphanage at the age of seven, and sentenced to the Texas State Penitentiary at the age of nineteen, James Ryle's life is a powerful and uplifting story of how God's grace can work all things together for good. His ability to connect with people of all ages, combined with a keen sense of humour and sensitivity make James one of the most sought after speakers today. His is a seasoned voice that brings moral clarity and refreshing insights for people of all walks of life.

James Ryle is the President and Founder of TruthWorks Ministries, a teaching and resourcing ministry helping individuals live real, relevant and significant lives for Christ. He has been involved in public speaking since 1972, serving as pastor of two churches, chaplain for the University of Colorado football team, and ministering as an evangelist, Bible teacher and popular conference speaker throughout the USA and abroad. He is a best-selling author, and a contributor to both the *NKJV Spirit Filled Life Bible*, and the *NIV Worship Leader's Bible*.

James is one of the founding Board members of Promise Keepers, and has spoken at multiple PK stadium events around the USA. On October 4, 1997, James delivered the gospel message at Stand in the Gap, an event attended by over 1.4 million men, and broadcast to over 20 different nations around the world.

James and his wife, Belinda, have four grown children and currently live in Tennessee.